SMARTCUTS

SMARTCUTS

*How Hackers, Innovators,
and Icons Accelerate Success*

SHANE SNOW

HARPER
BUSINESS

An Imprint of HarperCollins*Publishers*

HarperCollins books may be purchased for educational, business, or sales promotional use. For information, please e-mail the Special Markets Department at SPsales@harpercollins.com.

FIRST EDITION

Designed by Renato Stanisic

Library of Congress Cataloging-in-Publication Data has been applied for.

ISBN 978-0-06-230245-8

14 15 16 17 18   OV/RRD   10 9 8 7 6 5 4 3 2 1

CONTENTS

SMARTCUTS

INTRODUCTION

"How Do They Move So Fast?"

On a blustery winter morning in early 2007, Nathan Parkinson broke the world record for the fastest completion of the classic video game *Super Mario Bros.* I watched him do it.*

We were in Rexburg, Idaho, a college town of 25,000 people, and Nate was definitely supposed to be in class. I emerged from my bedroom that morning, backpack in hand, to the usual sight. Blinds closed. Lights off. The unnatural glow from our 20-inch television in the corner. And Nate, about a foot away from the screen.

He would sit cross-legged, glasses fixed atop his nose, thin blond hair standing on end, held straight by weeks of oil buildup. His best friend and backseat driver, Tommy, would perch scrawny and shirtless on the armrest, after a night of snoozing rent-free on our couch in between turns at the game system.

Nate and Tommy routinely said good-bye to me at 8:00 a.m. as I left for Economics class, and I knew they still had an hour or two of *GameCube* left in them. But that day they were playing on an old-school Nintendo system—which was odd—and that day Tommy had video recording equipment set up.

---

* And you can, too, at shanesnow.com/mario.

"Nate's trying to beat the world record for Mario one," Tommy informed me.

I sat down to watch.

BUNDLED WITH THE ORIGINAL Nintendo Entertainment System in 1986, *Super Mario Bros.* ushered in the modern video gaming era. With 40 million copies sold, it became a staple of '80s pop culture and held the honor of the "world's best-selling video game" for two decades.

Super Mario Bros. has 32 levels, or missions, making up a total of eight "worlds." Each world has new scenery, different obstacles, and progressively badder bad guys. Each level has a time limit of 400 game seconds, which are a bit shorter than actual seconds. In theory, the game should take between one and two hours to beat, assuming you don't die.

Until moves and timing are mastered, Mario is incredibly frustrating; touching a bad guy or falling into one of the countless pits spattering the landscape resets the level. After three chances, or "lives," the game restarts.

At the time I sat down to watch Nate play the game, 22 years after its release, the standing world record for completing all the levels of *Super Mario Bros.* was 33 minutes, 24 seconds.

When Nate cleared the final level that day in Idaho, dumping the final boss, Bowser, into a pit of lava and signifying the end of the game, Tommy's stopwatch read six minutes, 28 seconds.

Wait . . .

HOW DO YOU BEAT the world's most played video game in one-fifth of world-record time?

As only someone who spent his or her childhood mashing red plastic buttons together might guess, the answer is Warp Pipes.

Throughout *Super Mario Bros.*, Mario encounters a number of large green pipes. Some pipes are stopped up. Some pipes have evil plants living in them. And some pipes go to the sewer. Naturally, as a plumber, Mario likes to climb down these pipes, which lead to underground chambers where he can collect coins and mushrooms. The chambers invariably lead to more pipes, which take Mario back to the surface.

But the game creators also made a few secret pipes. These lead not to stinky sewers and disreputable fungi, but to new worlds, allowing Mario to skip levels by the dozen.

According to video game lore, these Warp Pipes were created so game testers could evaluate later levels without having to beat early worlds over and over again. Some, however, suspect these secret pipes were left as "Easter eggs" for fans to discover.

Nate didn't care about *why* the Warp Pipes were there; he just sent his Mario straight to them. He raced through Level 1-1, then broke a hole in the ceiling on Level 1-2 and ran full speed *on top of the level*, until he found the secret chamber with Warp Pipes to Worlds 2, 3, and 4.

Of course, Nate picked World 4.

Nate's Mario kept running, pausing only to eat a power-up mushroom, so he could race past a pair of "Hammer Brothers" and survive (this gambit got him through the bad guys in half the time). Soon, he was climbing a secret vine that led to the Warp Pipe for World 8, which he then had to beat manually.

He beat it. By this point, I'd scurried off to Econ, but I can only imagine the victory dance that ensued in our dingy apartment. After I came home and saw the tape, I promptly told everyone I knew.

Finishing *Super Mario Bros.* in six minutes using Warp Pipes isn't possible if you aren't truly good at *Super Mario Bros.* The warp doesn't mean you're going to win, or that you deserve to. It just means you don't have to slog through stages you already know you can beat.

This is not a book about video games, or the ensuing drama after Nate's record was sought, and overtaken, over the next few years.

This is a book about Warp Pipes in real life.

IT TOOK THE OIL tycoon John D. Rockefeller 46 years to make a billion dollars. He clawed his way to the top of the 19th-century business world. Starting with a single oil refinery in 1863, over two decades, he constructed oil pipelines and bought out rival refineries until he'd built an empire.

Seventy years later, the 1980s computer baron Michael Dell achieved billionaire status in 14 years; Bill Gates in 12. In the 1990s, Jerry Yang and David Filo of Yahoo each earned ten figures in just four years. It took Pierre Omidyar, founder of eBay, three years to do it. And in the late 2000s, Groupon's Andrew Mason did it in two.

Sure, there's been inflation since Rockefeller, but there's no disputing that we've decreased the time it takes innovative people to achieve dreams, get rich, and make an impact on the world—and this has largely been due to technology and communication.

"A serious assessment of the history of technology shows that technological change is exponential," writes the futurist and author Ray Kurzweil in his famous essay *The Law of Accelerating Returns.* "So we won't experience 100 years of progress in the 21st century—it will be more like 20,000 years of progress (at today's rate)." Here we come, *Star Trek*!

At the same time, many industries remain decidedly stuck in

the past. Most large businesses stop growing after a few years. Formal education, in many cases, is so slow or out-of-date that venture capitalists pay bright people to skip school and start Internet companies. Conventional wisdom—outside of the technology industry—on innovation and career building has hardly evolved since the 19th century.

We're multiplying our capabilities as a civilization and yet we still accept the notion that important societal progress, like combating inequality and crime—or even innovating in government and medicine—must take generations. Despite leaps in what we *can* do, most of us still follow comfortable, pre-prescribed paths. We work hard, but hardly question whether we're working smart.

On the other hand, some among us manage to build eBay in the time it takes the rest of us to build a house. Pick your era in history and you'll find a handful of people—across industries and continents—who buck the norm and do incredible things in implausibly short amounts of time. The common pattern is that, like computer hackers, certain innovators break convention to find better routes to stunning accomplishments.

The question is, can finding these better routes be taught?

PRETEND YOU ARE DRIVING a car in the middle of a thunderstorm and you happen upon three people on the side of the road. One of them is a frail old woman, who looks on the verge of collapse. Another is a friend who once saved your life. The other is the romantic interest of your dreams, and this is a once-in-a-lifetime opportunity to meet him or her. You have only one other seat in the car.

Who do you pick up?

There's a good reason to choose any of the three. The old woman needs help. The friend deserves your payback. And clearly, a happy future with the man or woman of your dreams will have an enormous long-term impact on your life.

So, who should you pick?

The old woman, of course. Then, give the car keys to your friend, and stay behind with the romantic interest to wait for the bus!

This dilemma is an exercise in lateral thinking. It's the kind of puzzle in which the most elegant solution is revealed only when you attack it sideways. New ideas emerge when you question the assumptions upon which a problem is based (in this case: it's that you can only help one person).

In this book, I'm going to show you how overachievers throughout history have applied lateral thinking to success in a variety of fields and endeavors. In doing this, I plan to convince you that the fastest route to success is never traditional, and that the conventions we grow up with can be hacked. And, most important, I want to show you that anyone—not just billionaire entrepreneurs and professional mavericks—can speed up progress in business or life.

But first, I'm going to share two quick stories to explain this book's title word, *smartcut*.

WHEN BENJAMIN FRANKLIN WAS 16 years old, he was a fantastic writer. He worked at his older brother James's printing shop for the newspaper the *New-England Courant*. Because his brother wouldn't print a boy's story, Ben began writing cultural essays under a pseudonym, Mrs. Silence Dogood, leaving them under the printshop door.

James published the letters in short order, and they were, in colonial terms, a smash hit. James and his friends thought a clever peer was writing the essays.

The letters became important to both the community and the paper. When Silence Dogood stopped writing in, James Franklin posted an ad:

If any person or persons will give a true account of Mrs. Silence Dogood, whether dead or alive, married or un-married, in town or countrey, that so, (if living) she may be spoke with, or letters convey'd to her, they shall have thanks for their pains.

When he found out who Silence really was, James was shocked. Ben left, taking his talents and publishing experience to Philadelphia, where he went on to become the most prolific inventor and states-man of the period. Here was an overachiever who didn't let conven-tion—in his case, age—stand in his way. When he was blocked from doing what he was capable of, he proved himself anyway.

Three hundred years later, another American boy—Frank Wil-liam Abagnale Jr.—also pretended to be someone he wasn't. His story, made famous by Steven Spielberg's *Catch Me If You Can*, in-volved a lot of hacking: impersonating lawyers and doctors, forg-ing checks, and traveling across continents as a fake airline pilot.

"Back then it truly was survival," Abagnale tells me, reminiscing. Despite how fabulous gallivanting around the world for free may sound, as his lies piled up, his definition of success shifted from fill-ing up bank accounts to simply not getting caught for another day.

"Then, I was sentenced to twelve years in federal prison."

The difference between Franklin's unconventional work and Abagnale's was that the former managed to create value for others while the latter cheated others. Franklin's approach was a lateral solution to the unfairness of present convention. Abagnale's, how-ever entertaining, was a con, and he paid for it.

And that's the difference between rapid, but short-term gains, which I call shortcuts, and sustainable success achieved quickly through smart work, or smartcuts. Whereas by dictionary definition shortcuts can be amoral, you can think of smartcuts as shortcuts with integrity. Working smarter and achieving more—without creating negative externalities.

Abagnale took shortcuts and regretted it. Franklin used smartcuts and got his face on a $100 bill.

After being released from prison, Abagnale spent three decades repaying his debt to society, working for the FBI, without pay. Eventually, he started a security business, met his future wife while on undercover assignment, and had three kids. "True success is not defined by how much money do I make, how well do I speak, how well do I deal with the subjects I deal with," he says. "But how great of a father I am."

As we explore the unconventional behavior of history's overachievers in *Smartcuts*, I hope we'll keep Abagnale's lesson in mind. To some people, success means wealth. To others it means recognition, popularity, or promotions; it means free time, inventing products, growing businesses, making breakthroughs at work. Those can all be good things, and in this book, we'll look at people and companies that achieved big things in the above categories. But I'm convinced that true success has more to do with our becoming better people and building a better world *while we do these things* than it does with the size of our bank accounts.

I STARTED WRITING ABOUT smartcuts—though not yet by that term—for *Fast Company* and other publications after moving to New York at a time when the city's tech community was starting to boom. As a budding reporter with time on my hands, I shadowed fast-growing startups like Foursquare as over the course of six months they grew from three guys with laptops to a million users, and Tumblr, whose 26-year-old founder cashed out for $1.1 billion after growing it to 100 million users. I hung out at hacker labs where people built Internet-connected robots out of used hospital machinery, and witnessed groups like the New York Tech Meetup surge from a few hundred to over 35,000 local members.

My writing led me to join several groups in that tech scene that I can only describe as "overachiever clubs," such as the Young Entrepreneur Council and the Sandbox Network (who actually call themselves "Overachievers Under 30")—kids who quit PhD programs and investment banking jobs to live on ramen and build things that could change the world.

You can't hang around these kinds of people without being inspired. Inevitably, I ended up cofounding a startup company of my own, which took me even further down the rabbit hole. (You can learn more about my company, Contently, at shanesnow.com/contently if you are interested.) Through that work, I soon found myself inducted into more groups: *Forbes*'s and *Inc.*'s 30 Under 30, TechStars, and NYC Venture Fellows—programs that put ambitious innovators together.

As if without warning, I found myself—a star-struck kid from Idaho—hanging out with incredible people, from the founders of world-changing companies to inventors whose life work was to solve unemployment in India or topple dictatorships. I was in a unique spot to observe—from the inside—people who were doing crazy things at implausibly young ages or in surprisingly fast times.

So, I wrote about them.

And I asked myself, how do they move so fast?

This book comes out of countless hours of research, hundreds of interviews, and the dissection of myriad academic papers in an effort to answer that question. Initially, I set out to discover the common patterns among rapidly successful tech companies, but I soon realized that their habits were simply permutations of principles smart people had been using in a variety of contexts throughout history.

I see this book as a simultaneous hat tip and counterpoint to some of the great success and innovation literature out there (check out shanesnow.com/booklist for my recommendations). It's a re-analysis and first codification of the ways *rapid* success has happened throughout history.

The step-by-step advice that made an ancient Greek hero rapidly prosperous will be entirely different from what makes a 21st-century businesswoman successful, just as the exact methods an Internet startup uses to grow today will be irrelevant in five years. But the patterns of lateral thinking (smartcuts) behind each of their success stories can be harnessed by anyone who seeks an edge—at work, at the gym, in the arts or education, from social enterprise to personal development, from big companies to small startups.

In each of the following chapters, we'll explore one of those patterns. I've divided the nine of them into three classes, which make up the three parts of this book:

SHORTEN

Earlier, we discussed the scenario of the old woman in the thunderstorm. Were you surprised that the path to the most success in that scenario involved stepping outside and getting rain soaked?

This is the kind of thinking that computer scientists—and especially computer hackers—use. Got two short Internet cables but need one long one? Cut the ends off and splice the two together. Want to digitize libraries of old books without typing them up yourself? Get millions of people on the Internet to do it for you. (Ever filled out those crazy letters—called CAPTCHAs—when you signed up for something online? That's what you're doing.)

Increasingly in today's culture, "hacking" is something done not just by criminals and computer scientists, but by anyone who has the capability to approach a problem laterally. (This is the original usage of the term, in fact.) Can't get that horrible plastic "blister pak" for those headphones open? Use a can opener. (It works!)

Not enough seats for the four of you? Give yours up and weather the storm with the person of your dreams.

The first section of this book discusses how some people use such "hacker" thinking to *shorten* paths to success. It's how some people take a few years to become president while others spend 30. It's how unknown comedians get on *Saturday Night Live* and Internet companies get to millions of users in months.

Lateral thinking doesn't replace hard work; it eliminates unnecessary cycles. Once they've shortened their path, overachievers tend to look for ways to do more with their effort, which brings us to our next section:

LEVERAGE

Pretend you're fixing up an old house, and you need to pry a nail out of the wood floor in the living room. You have a claw hammer, but try as you can, the nail won't come out.

You have a few options at this point. You could give up (maybe pulling the nail is unnecessary), but let's assume it's essential we get this nail out. One option is to exert more force, pull harder. Maybe if your life depended on it, you could work the nail out over a long period of time. But then you'll be too tired to sand the floor.

This is what the classic success advice amounts to: work 100 hours a week, believe you can do it, visualize, and push yourself harder than everyone else. Claw that nail out with your bare hands 'til they bleed if necessary. This is *the hard way*.

Or maybe you can admit defeat and phone your biggest friend, so he can come over and give the nail pulling a shot. That's less work for you, but suddenly, you've created more *net* work. And what if there's not one, but 70 nails to pull? This is the other common success advice: outsource the tough stuff, and try to profit from the arbitrage. This is *the cheap way.*

The easiest solution in this case, however, is not to waste energy, not to bother your friend, but to find a long piece of pipe to put over the hammer's handle and to push on the end of the pipe. The toughest nail will pop out. The law of the lever, as shown by the Greek mathematician Archimedes, says the longer the lever, the less force you need exert.

This is *the smart way.*

Leverage is the overachiever's approach to getting more bang for her proverbial buck. It's how brand-new startups scale and young sci-fi geeks become movie directors. It's how below-average school systems turn around and revolutions are won. It's how surfers take championships and artists go from homeless to the Grammys.

SOAR

I'm not much of an athlete, but there's one sport in which I feel it's all right to brag about my abilities for a minute: monkey bars, circa age ten.

When I was a shrimpy, red-headed kid on the primary school playground, my arms were too short to reach the Olympic rings, a series of circular handles hanging by chains at the jungle gym. You're supposed to hang from the handles and work your way across the span, hand over hand.

Though the gap between handles was wider than my wing-span, I learned to navigate them like a real Olympian: by grabbing one handle and swinging with all my might toward the next one, so the chain became a pendulum that took me to the next handle. Once I started swinging, however, I couldn't stop, or I'd get stuck, spread-eagled between two rings. So I swung and swung, never holding two handles at once, until I reached the end.

My adventures on the monkey bars are analogous to the smartcuts that we'll discuss in the final third of the book. These principles explain how rocketeers and makeup artists defy expectations and become world-class icons. They're how tech geeks save lives and community college flunkies catalyze global change.

And they're how regular people can make their dreams happen, regardless how short their arms are.

SOME OF THE IDEAS in this book are subversive. I'm not being contrarian for the sake of it; I'm hoping to spark lateral thinking when it comes to success, indeed to show that lateral thinking is how the *most* successful people have always made it.

In the following chapters, I'll explain why kids shouldn't be taught multiplication tables, where the fashionable "fail fast and fail often" mantra of the Lean Startup movement breaks down, and how momentum—not experience—is the single biggest predictor of business and personal success. I'll debunk our common myths about mentorship and paying dues. And I'll show why, paradoxically, it's easier to build a huge business than a small one.

Good fortune and talent are both ingredients of success, but like any recipe, they can be substituted with clever alternatives. The one irreplaceable ingredient I've found, however, is work. This book is not a how-to guide, nor is it for people who don't want to work hard or who want to build easy businesses. This book is about patterns found in stories of people who didn't want their hard work to end up in vain, who were too impatient to accept "that's just how it's done."

Too many of us place our hopes and dreams in the unreliable hands of luck, but the world's most rapidly successful people take luck into their own hands (even though many are too humble to say so). Too many of us accept the plateaus our lives have offered us and succumb to passivity, to the well-meaning delusion of "If I work hard enough, something good will hopefully happen to me."

By the end of this book, I'd like to convince you that serendipity can be engineered, that luck can be manufactured, convention can be defied, and that the best paths to success—no matter how you define it—are different today from what they were yesterday.

Sᴉxᴛᴇᴇɴ ᴍᴏɴᴛʜs ᴀꜰᴛᴇʀ ᴛʜᴀᴛ record-breaking morning in Rexburg, Idaho, some guy named Ashton beat Nate's *Mario* time by 26 seconds. (Nate actually had to restart the last level of his speed run; a flying turtle killed him, or else he'd have shaved a.ı-other half-minute off his time.) Today's world record for *Super Mario Bros.* is five minutes, eight seconds, held by Scott Kessler. I'm sure someone will beat his score, too.

What does the world's youngest Nobel Prize winner have in common with a world-class children's hospital? What do the fastest-growing media companies in the world, top heart surgeons, and young US presidents do to get to the front of the pack? What can we learn from electronic music sensations, sneaker designers, and amateur rocket scientists that has anything to do with our day-to-day ambitions as workers, dreamers, and business builders?

The answer is, *a lot more than we think.*

PART I

SHORTEN

You have brains in your head. You have feet in your shoes.
You can steer yourself any direction you choose.

—Dr. Seuss

Chapter 1

HACKING THE LADDER

"Bored Mormons"

I.

A strange thing has been happening in the United States for nearly 300 years. For some reason, our presidents are younger than our senators.

The average president of the United States takes office at age 55. In contrast, US senators start their terms in Congress—the most recent at the time of this writing—at an average of age 62. Members of the House of Representatives were 57.

This is not a recent anomaly. Presidents have tended to be younger than Congress since the Founding Fathers died. And though a handful began the job as senior citizens, the average starting age has never crossed 60.

These statistics are especially peculiar because of how much more difficult it is to become president than a senator. Terms in the Senate are commonly seen as a *step* on the path to president. But even brand-new senators, holding their first federal office ever, have been coming in at an average of 56 and 57 in recent years. Presidents get to the top before senators get in the door.

Why?

Armchair explanations like good looks don't make sense. Why would we be more likely to vote for a handsome young president but not a good-looking young congressperson? Data in presidential versus congressional elections indicates that youth voter turnout isn't the culprit.

Some sort of creeping mistrust of the elderly or the advent of televised elections aren't skewing the results, either. The oldest-elected president, Ronald Reagan, took office at age 69, with the fourth-oldest, George H. W. Bush, succeeding him at 64. They brought up the average. Gerrymandering and changing campaign finance laws don't seem to explain the data, and the *losers* in presidential elections actually tend to be the same average age as the winners.

We've had rich presidents, poor presidents, political-insider presidents, Washington-outsider presidents, pretty presidents, ugly presidents, eloquent presidents, stammering presidents, old presidents, and young presidents. But mostly young presidents.

Lyndon B. Johnson became president at exactly 55. Perhaps his story will give us a clue to the phenomenon.

Born on a farm in Texas, Johnson was always a talker. He first ran for president in 11th grade. He won. Described by peers as ambitious from the beginning, he got involved in adult politics shortly after high school. He first served as a legislative secretary to a Texas congressman, but had won his own seat in the US House by age 29. Several terms later, he moved up to the Senate. From junior senator he rose to the rank of majority whip, then minority leader, then majority leader. Having paid his dues in each branch of Congress, he was elected John F. Kennedy's vice president in 1960.

Then, tragically, President Kennedy was killed, and LBJ assumed his office, having climbed the political ladder for 25 years.

From the beginning of his career, LBJ was extraordinarily focused. He worked hard, pulled himself up by his own bootstraps, and patiently worked the ladder. And, after all that work, the last stage of his ascent came down to luck. If Kennedy had lived, Vice President Johnson wouldn't have had the chance to run for president until he was in his 60s.

We all know this ladder-climbing story. It's gospel we've preached in career- and business-building for centuries. We're told that the best way to succeed is to start young, work hard, and move up through the ranks. The two ingredients are hard work—not quitting when things get tough—and luck—spots opening up on the rungs above you. LBJ's is that quintessential American story.

The problem is, when we look at the data, LBJ's isn't the quintessential *presidential* story at all.

Only three other presidents out of the 43 people who have been president at the time of this writing climbed the rungs of all four elected federal offices: Richard Nixon, Andrew Johnson, and John Tyler. Just over half of the presidents were ever congressmen at all.

It gets even more interesting when we look at the amount of time these men spent climbing up the political ladder. The ten oldest presidents—the ones who bring our age average up—held a federal office for nine years,* or less than two Senate terms. Lyndon B. Johnson's story would suggest that these older presidents fought their way up the congressional ladder over a quarter century, and just got started a little later. But no.

In fact, most presidents spent just over half as many years in state and federal politics as LBJ did. Ignoring state politics, the average president spent just seven years as an elected official before reaching the White House. Five were never elected to *any* office before becoming president.

---

* Excluding political appointments. And Gerald Ford's 25 years in federal politics skews the average; the median is seven.

There's something wrong with the great American ladder-climbing advice: presidents of the United States, some of the world's most successful people, don't follow it.

It's like each invented his own ladder.

II.

There is a pattern to the unconventional career tracks of US presidents. We find it among other groups as well. Throughout history, fast-rising companies, rock-star executives, "overnight" movie stars, and top-selling products have outrun their peers by acting more like ladder hackers than ladder climbers.

The best way to explain how that ladder hacking works comes from the Mormons.

RELATIVELY FEW PEOPLE LIVE in the environs of Brigham Young University, out in the American West. Some who do are occasionally surprised by a late-night knock on the front door and a strange request. Not from preachers or salesmen, but from bored Mormon college students.

Mormons—and Mormon schools like BYU—have a health code that discourages alcohol. When you put tens of thousands of young abstainers together in a small college town, an obnoxious proliferation of creative group activities results. One of them is the reason for that late-night knock. It's a game called Bigger or Better.

Bigger or Better is a scavenger hunt, a sort of trick-or-treating for (young) adults. Players divide into teams and begin with a small object, like a toothpick, then disperse and knock on neighborhood doors, one house after another.

At each answered door, the players introduce themselves with something on the order of, "We're playing a game called Bigger or Better. Do you have something in your house that's slightly bigger or better than this . . ." (display object) " . . . that you would trade with us?"

The first few houses are the toughest. People relaxing *at* night in their homes aren't often *searching for* toothpicks. Even in the friendly Rocky Mountains a homeowner can be put off by such a request. But before long, a stranger will good-naturedly offer a piece of gum for that toothpick, and the game is on.

At the next house, the gum becomes a ballpoint pen. At the next: a pack of Post-it notes. Then: a copy of last month's *Nylon* magazine. The magazine becomes a bouquet of flowers left by an unwanted admirer. The flowers get swapped for an old hat, and the hat is exchanged for a novelty T-shirt. In this phase of the game, the players benefit from a bit of curiosity, a little charity, and the fact that people were planning on getting rid of most of these objects anyway.

But after enough trades, the players hold objects of significant value in their hands. Now the boy who opens the door sincerely wants the T-shirt. He trades his lava lamp for it. The girls next door like the lava lamp and decide to part with a vintage mirror. The old woman down the street collects antiques; she accepts the mirror in exchange for an old BMX bike in the garage.

When time is up, the players return home to compare results. After a dozen or so trades, teams have turned toothpicks into a stereo system, a set of golf clubs, and a television set. One group even drags in a full-size canoe.*

Not bad, for a sober night out.

---

* These are all actual winnings reported to me by Brigham Young students. There's even a myth that someone once brought back a used car in Bigger or Better. And in 2005, a little farther north, a young Canadian man named Kyle MacDonald famously played an Internet-based game of Bigger or Better where he started with a red paperclip and eventually traded up to a house after 12 months and 14 trades.

Bigger or Better illustrates an interesting fact: people are generally willing to take a chance on something if it only feels like a *small* stretch. That's how a group of bored students transformed a toothpick into a TV, and remarkably quicker than if they'd worked their seven-dollar-per-hour college-town jobs and saved up for one. With each trade, the players exchanged or provided value—including entertainment value.

Now, if the BYU kids had gone door-to-door asking for free televisions, they wouldn't have succeeded so quickly. Few people are willing to make that kind of stretch. This is like an intern applying for a CEO job, or a brand-new startup bidding on a NASA contract. The players eliminated resistance by breaking the big challenge (acquire something valuable like a TV) into a series of easier, repeatable challenges (make a tiny trade).

Researchers call this the psychology of "small wins." Gamblers, on the other hand, would call it a "parlay," which the dictionary defines as "a cumulative series of bets in which winnings accruing from each transaction are used as a stake for a further bet."

In Bigger or Better, the parlay never stops. Players don't wait an arbitrary period of time before moving on to the next trade, and they don't mind if the result of a trade was only a *slightly* more desirable object, so long as the game keeps moving.

"By itself, one small win may seem unimportant," writes Dr. Karl Weick in a seminal paper for *American Psychologist* in 1984. "A series of wins at small but significant tasks, however, reveals a pattern that may attract allies, deter opponents, and *lower resistance to subsequent proposals.*"

"Once a small win has been accomplished," Weick continues, "forces are set in motion that favor another small win."

From the outside, this simply seems like a prudent way to climb the ladder: as fast as possible,* and in small bites.

---

* For a deeper read on this, visit shanesnow.com/cycletime.

While that's good advice, the key to the bored Mormon students' success was not just their rapid cycle time. It was the direction they traded: *sideways.*

The players didn't simply parlay toothpicks for pieces of wood of increasing size; they traded toothpicks for pens and mirrors for old bikes. They didn't wait around for the owners of a vacant house to show up, so they could ask for a trade, and they didn't knock on the same door over and over until a "no" became a "yes." When a door was shut to them, they immediately picked another one. When the ladder became inefficient, they hacked it. And *that* is what made them successful so quickly.

The key to Bigger or Better, in other words, is the "or."

THE FASTEST LAND ANIMAL in the world is the cheetah. It can reach speeds in excess of 70 miles per hour. But, according to behavioral biologists, speed is not the cheetah's biggest predatory advantage. As science writer Katie Hiler puts it, "It is their agility—their skill at leaping sideways, changing directions abruptly and slowing down quickly—that gives those antelope such bad odds."

When we look at fast success in business and other fields, we see this cheetah behavior everywhere: One of the fastest-selling and transformative cellular phones in the world—the iPhone— was introduced by a personal computer company, at a time when the phone market was dominated by telecommunications firms. Nintendo began its life printing Japanese playing cards; the company brokered in taxis, instant rice, and hotels before it saw opportunity in the emerging American arcade scene. The novelist James Patterson, whose books have sold 275 million copies at last count, was an ad executive before switching over to literature (and leveraging his marketing expertise to become a bestseller).

Award-winning actress Zoe Saldana was a ballet dancer before becoming a movie star. (Her first role was a ballet dancer.) This is often how "overnight success" happens for entertainers and public figures; they work hard in their field, then switch ladders and level up, to observers' surprise.

Business research shows that this kind of ladder switching generally tends to accelerate a company's growth. Companies that pivot—that is, switch business models or products—while on the upswing tend to perform much better than those that stay on a single course. The 2011 Startup Genome Report of new technology companies states that, "Startups that pivot once or twice raise 2.5x more money, have 3.6x better user growth, and are 52% less likely to scale prematurely."

LET'S TAKE A DEEPER look at the fastest-climbing US presidents. The ones who bring *down* the average time spent on the political ladder. Here they are:

President	Years in Elected Political Office	President	Years in Elected Political Office
Zachary Taylor	0	Abraham Lincoln	2
Ulysses S. Grant	0	Grover Cleveland	5
Herbert Hoover	0	George W. Bush	5
William Howard Taft	0	Franklin D. Roosevelt	5
Dwight D. Eisenhower	0	Rutherford B. Hayes	7
George Washington	1	Jimmy Carter	8
Chester Arthur	1	Ronald Reagan	8
Woodrow Wilson	2		

Here we have one-third of our presidents, most of whom had less time in elected office than it takes to get a political science degree.

Now let's look at what they did before president:

President	Occupation(s) Prior to Presidency
Zachary Taylor	US Army Lieutenant > Major General > President
Ulysses S. Grant	Soldier > Leather Worker > US Army General > President
Herbert Hoover	Philanthropist > Secretary of Commerce > President
William Howard Taft	Prosecutor > Judge > Governor-General of the Philippines > Secretary of War > President
Dwight D. Eisenhower	Military Officer > WWII Supreme Allied Commander > University President > President
George Washington	Continental Congress Delegate > General > President
Chester Arthur	New York Port Collector > Vice President > President
Woodrow Wilson	University President > Governor > President
Abraham Lincoln	State Legislator > Congressman > Prairie Lawyer > President
Grover Cleveland	Sheriff > Mayor > Governor > President
George W. Bush	Businessman > Governor > President
Franklin D. Roosevelt	State Senator > Assistant Secretary of the Navy > Governor > President
Rutherford B. Hayes	Military Officer > Congressman > Governor > President
Jimmy Carter	Peanut Farmer > State Senator > Governor > President
Ronald Reagan	Actor > Governor > President

The first thing you'll notice is that no two presidents in this group had the same climb up the ladder. You may have also noticed that there are a lot of military men in this list. And governors, too.

Then there are some weird ones. Philanthropist? University president? Actor?

Many of these men did have political savvy. William Howard Taft, for example, came from a well-connected family, and his eight-plus-rung ladder climb involved being collector of internal revenue in Cincinnati and governor of the US-occupied Philippines. But this is certainly not the expected path to president.

The common pattern among these fastest-rising US presidents' journeys is that, like the BYU students, they didn't parlay up a linear path. They climbed various ladders of success and then *switched to the presidential ladder.*

It's clear that switching ladders can help bypass "dues" and accelerate the Bigger or Better cycle. But what makes someone willing to make that sideways trade with us in the first place?

What about a general or a philanthropist makes us willing to make him our president?

III.

If there was ever a US president who stayed the course, it was Andrew Johnson. For 13 years, he paid his dues in Tennessee as mayor, state representative, and state senator. He spent ten years in the US House, four years as governor of Tennessee, five years as US senator, three years as military governor of Tennessee during the Civil War, and finally, vice president under Abraham Lincoln, who needed a Southerner in the White House to help unify the crumbling nation.

When Lincoln was assassinated, Johnson, one of the presidents with the longest political careers in history, assumed the presidency at age 56.

And then he proceeded to screw up.

Johnson was handed the high office at a time when America

was bruised and needed a good leader. But Johnson, despite his experience, was not a good leader. He was backward and racist, consistently undermined by his own inner circle, and he would have certainly botched America's post–Civil War reconstruction if only Congress had let him. The first president to be impeached, Johnson was the antithesis of the cheetah.

Historian James Ford Rhodes writes that Johnson "worked in a groove. Obstinate rather than firm it undoubtedly seemed to him that following counsel and making concessions were a display of weakness."

This was a man too stubborn to adapt. Though he spent more time in politics than nearly any other president, historians rank him as the second worst ever.

Clearly, paying his dues did not qualify him for the job.

It seems fair for success to be determined not by the hardworking but broken model of paying dues, but by merit and smarts. And we'd rather have presidents like Abe Lincoln than Andrew Johnson. But how are we to determine who's fit for the job, if not through past experience?

FOR HUNDREDS OF YEARS, people from every corner of the planet have flocked to New York City for the reason Frank Sinatra immortalized: to prove they could "make it." The allure, the prestige, the struggle to survive, breeds a brand, an image of the city that ripples out to the rest of the world. Sinatra sang about proving himself to himself. "If I can make it there, I'll make it anywhere." New York was the yardstick.

New York has indeed become a global yardstick—for artists, businesspeople, and dreamers of all stripes. *He was a lawyer in New York? He must be good.* Doesn't matter if he was the worst lawyer in the city. If you can make it in New York, people assume that you can make it anywhere.

The yardstick the public uses when judging a presidential candidate, it turns out, is not how much time the candidate has in politics. "It's leadership qualities," explains the presidential historian Doug Wead, a former adviser to George H. W. Bush and the author of 30 books on the presidents. Indeed, polls indicate that being "a strong and decisive leader" is the number one characteristic a presidential candidate can have.

The fastest-climbing presidents, it turns out, used the Sinatra Principle to convey their leadership cred. What shows leadership like commanding an army (Washington), running a university (Wilson), governing a state for a few years—even if you started out as an actor (Reagan)—or building a new political party and having the humility to put aside your own interests for the good of the whole (Lincoln)?

Dwight D. Eisenhower led the United States and its allies to victory against Hitler. He had never held an elected office. He won by a landslide with five times the electoral votes of his rival. "If he can make it there, he can make it anywhere," US voters decided.

IV.

The presidents, for the most part, got to high office by not playing the game everyone else plays. They acquire leadership experience in disparate fields, then use Frank Sinatra–style credibility to switch ladders to politics.

There's one remaining question, however. We've seen how dues and experience are bad proxies for ability or merit. But does bypassing dues and experience leave us without the necessary skill to do the job? The Sinatra Principle helps presidents get the job, but does it qualify them for it?

Why don't we ask the ten top-rated presidents in history:*

President	Years in Elected Office	Previous Occupation
Abraham Lincoln	2	Party Builder
George Washington	1	General
Franklin D. Roosevelt	5	Assistant Secretary of the Navy
Teddy Roosevelt	8	Sheriff
Harry S. Truman	11	Judge
John F. Kennedy	14	Soldier, Author
Thomas Jefferson	13	Lawyer, Revolutionary
Dwight D. Eisenhower	0	War Hero
Woodrow Wilson	2	University President
Ronald Reagan	8	Actor

All ten of the top ten presidents in C-SPAN's survey were hackers. Only one, JFK, climbed a semblance of a traditional ladder; he served in both houses of Congress, but was a war hero and author of a Pulitzer Prize–winning book—clearly not the average ladder climber. Each of the men on this list worked hard in his career, learned and proved leadership through diverse experiences, and switched ladders multiple times. They continuously parlayed their current success for something more, and they didn't give up when they lost elections (which most of them did).

The ladder switching made them better at getting elected and

---

* Dates approximate, especially for pre-Revolutionary War officeholders.

better at the job. To be a good president, Wead says, "You've got to be able to think on your feet." Stubbornness and tradition make for poor performance—as we see with Andrew Johnson and other presidents at the bottom of history's rankings.

The fact that our best presidents—and history's other greatest overachievers—circumvented the system to get to the top speaks to what's wrong with our conventional wisdom of paying dues and climbing the ladder. Hard work and luck are certainly ingredients of success, but they're not the entire recipe.

Senators and representatives, by contrast, generally play the dues-and-ladder game of hierarchy and formality. And they get stuck in the congressional spiderweb. "The people that go into Congress go step by step by step," Wead explains.

But presidents don't.

It begs the question: should we?

WE LIVE IN AN age of nontraditional ladder climbing. Not just in politics, but in business and personal development and education and entertainment and innovation. Traditional paths are not just slow; they're no longer viable if we want to compete and innovate.

That's great news, because throwing out the dues paradigm leads us toward meritocracy. But to be successful, we need to start thinking more like hackers, acting more like entrepreneurs. We have to work smarter, not just harder.

We'll see throughout the following chapters how Sinatra-style credibility and ladder switching—always parlaying for something more—are the foundation for how the most interesting people and companies in the world succeed. It's not just how presidents get to the top. It's how CEOs and comedians and racecar drivers hone their skills and make it in the big leagues. It's how new businesses grow fast, and old businesses grow faster. It's how entrepreneurs create life-changing products in record time and inventors parlay dreams for bigger dreams.

Hacking the ladder is the mind-set they use to get places. The rest of this book is about becoming good enough to deserve it.

Chapter 2

TRAINING WITH MASTERS

"The Vocal Thief"

I.

The kid was nervous.

He stood on a small stage on Second Avenue, in the heart of the Upper East Side of Manhattan. Feet away from him sat Lorne Michaels, the gatekeeper to the world's most prestigious comedy clique and creator of the most Emmy-nominated television show in history. With dark eyes and short, salt-and-pepper hair, the man sat in a wooden chair and waited, silent and scrutinizing, expressionless as he usually was at times like this.

It was 1996, and this was The Comic Strip, the oldest stand-up comedy showcase club in New York City. The long-haired kid wore jeans and a pullover T-shirt, and held in his shaking hands a Troll doll, a plastic, pantsless toy with beady eyes and neon hair.

It was a rare audition for NBC's weekly sketch comedy series, *Saturday Night Live*. With The Comic Strip's iconic brick wall to his back—where Eddie Murphy and a hundred other superstar comics had cast their shadows over the years—and with a cluster of veteran comedy producers to his front, the kid stood, feet rooted to the spot where he was about to spend the scariest three minutes of his life.

Then the kid—Jimmy Fallon—took a breath, and began his routine.

ABOUT NINE MONTHS EARLIER, Randi Siegel, a feisty, up-and-coming talent manager, was starting a new job. She'd gotten her feet wet in the comedy industry working with stars like David Spade and Adam Sandler, and had, by age 26, worked herself into the *SNL* in crowd.

One day, a colleague named Peter Iselin, who'd recently moved to L.A. from Upstate New York, handed Siegel an audition tape.

"There's this kid," he told her—one of his former interns from his last job. "He's really great with impressions, and he wants to be on *Saturday Night Live*."

Get in line, Siegel thought. *So does everyone else.*

But she watched the tape anyway.

The five-minute home video showed a teenage Jimmy performing at a small comedy club. The bit was a pretend audition held by a Troll doll that was seeking a spokesman. Various characters, voiced by Jimmy, "auditioned" for the "job," including a convincing faux–Jerry Seinfeld.

"He was adorable," Siegel recalls. "Very, very green. He was this nervous kid. But talent shines through, and he clearly had that."

She asked for Jimmy's phone number.

A FEW DAYS LATER, Siegel stayed late at the office and dialed long-distance.

"Hi," she said. "I'm looking for Jimmy Fallon."

"This is Jimmy Fallon," announced a hyper-sounding 20-year-old on the other end.

"Oh. This is Randi Siegel—"

"Randi Siegel! I know who you are!"

This was not the response she expected. It turned out that while his peers at St. Rose College memorized NFL rosters and the names of their favorite rock band drummers, Jimmy had tirelessly followed his heroes in comedy. He fixated on the careers of comics like Sandler and Spade and tracked the movements of their management teams, agencies, films, and TV shows as if he was earning school credit for it.

Jimmy's goal since childhood, he explained to Siegel, had been to join the cast of *Saturday Night Live*.

He was endearing. After a two-hour call, Siegel offered to represent him. She had one question, however.

"Why don't you stay and graduate?" Jimmy was a semester shy of a degree. Siegel suggested that they get started in the summer, so he'd have a bachelor's degree to fall back on, just in case.

"No, no," Jimmy insisted. "I need to get on *Saturday Night Live*, and you're going to make it happen, because you know Adam Sandler! I don't want to do anything else."

Siegel knew this was a long shot—and a long-term endeavor—especially for an out-of-town kid with zero acting credits. But for some reason, she couldn't turn him down; she had never met someone as focused and passionate about a single dream as this grinning bumpkin from the tiny town of Saugerties, New York. And though his skills were rough, given some time in the industry, she thought he might just make it.

"OK, let's do this," she said.

So, in January 1996 Jimmy quit college and moved to Los Angeles. For six months, Siegel booked him gigs on small, local stand-up comedy stages. Then, without warning, *SNL* put a call out for auditions; three cast members would be leaving the show. Having worked with one of the departing actors, David Spade,

Siegel pulled a few strings and arranged a Hail Mary for the young Jimmy Fallon: an audition at The Comic Strip.

SO HERE HE WAS. Fresh-faced, sweating in his light shirt, holding his Troll doll. In front of Lorne Michaels and a phalanx of Hollywood shakers.

When Jimmy ended his three-minute bit, the audience clapped politely. True to his reputation, Michaels didn't laugh. Not once. Jimmy went home and awaited word.

Finally, the results came: *SNL* had invited Tracy Morgan, Ana Gasteyer, and Chris Kattan, each of whom had hustled in the comedy scene for years, to join the cast. Jimmy—the newbie whose well-connected manager had finagled an invite—was crushed.

"Was he completely raw? A hundred percent," Siegel says.

But, the *SNL* people said, "Let's keep an eye on him."

II.

If you don't live under a rock, you probably know that Jimmy Fallon eventually became one of comedy's fastest-rising icons and the host of the prestigious *Tonight Show* by age 38. This chapter is about how he ultimately shortened his path to Hollywood success.

Many entertainers toil for decades to get their break. They pay their Actors Guild dues, hone their craft, and starve like artists until they reach a tipping point. Funnyman Louis C.K., for example, spent 15 years performing stand-up comedy for ungrateful local crowds before finally catching his break and becoming a recognizable name with his own cable TV series.

On the other hand, some people skip the dues and jump straight to the top, like the Canadian singer Justin Bieber, who played a few songs on YouTube and became an international megastar in a year. Bieber's first record went platinum; his first single went diamond; his second and third records each hit number one by the time he was eighteen.

Both C.K. and Bieber are extremely gifted performers. Both climbed to the top of their industry, and in fact, both ultimately used the Internet to get big. But somehow Bieber "made it" in one-fifteenth of the time.

How did he climb so much faster than the guy *Rolling Stone* calls the funniest man in America—and what does this have to do with Jimmy Fallon?

The answer begins with a story from Homer's *Odyssey*.

When the Greek adventurer Odysseus embarked for war with Troy, he entrusted his son, Telemachus, to the care of a wise old friend named Mentor. Mentor raised and coached Telemachus in his father's absence.

But it was really the goddess Athena disguised as Mentor who counseled the young man through various important situations. Through Athena's training and wisdom, Telemachus soon became a great hero.

"Mentor" helped Telemachus shorten his ladder of success.

The simple answer to the Bieber question is that the young singer shot to the top of pop with the help of two music industry mentors. And not just any run-of-the-mill coach, but R&B giant Usher Raymond and rising-star manager Scooter Braun. They reached from the top of the ladder where they were and pulled Bieber up, where his talent could be recognized by a wide audience. They helped him polish his performing skills, and in four years Bieber had sold 15 million records and been named by *Forbes* as the third most powerful celebrity in the world. Without Raymond's and Braun's mentorship, Biebs would probably still be playing acoustic guitar back home in Canada. He'd be hustling on his own just like Louis C.K., begging for attention amid a throng of hopeful entertainers.

Mentorship is the secret of many of the highest-profile achievers throughout history. Socrates mentored young Plato, who in turn mentored Aristotle. Aristotle mentored a boy named Alexander, who went on to conquer the known world as Alexander the Great.

From *The Karate Kid* to *Star Wars* to *The Matrix*, adventure stories often adhere to a template in which a protagonist forsakes humble beginnings and embarks on a great quest. Before the quest heats up, however, he or she receives training from a master: Obi Wan Kenobi. Mr. Miyagi. Mickey Goldmill. Haymitch. Morpheus. Quickly, the hero is ready to face overwhelming challenges. Much more quickly than if he'd gone to light-saber school.

The mentor story is so common because it seems to work—especially when the mentor is not just a teacher, but someone who's traveled the road herself. "A master can help you accelerate things," explains Jack Canfield, author of the *Chicken Soup for the Soul* series and career coach behind the bestseller *The Success Principles*. He says that, like C.K., we can spend thousands of hours practicing until we master a skill, or we can convince a world-class practitioner to guide our practice and cut the time to mastery significantly.

Research from Brunel University shows that chess students who trained with coaches increased on average 168 points in their national ratings versus those who didn't. Though long hours of deliberate practice are unavoidable in the cognitively complex arena of chess, the presence of a coach for mentorship gives players a clear advantage. Chess prodigy Joshua Waitzkin (the subject of the film *Searching for Bobby Fischer*) for example, accelerated his career when national chess master Bruce Pandolfini discovered him playing chess in Washington Square Park in New York as a boy. Pandolfini coached young Waitzkin one on one, and the boy won a slew of chess championships, setting a world record at an implausibly young age.

Business research backs this up, too. Analysis shows that entrepreneurs who have mentors end up raising seven times as much capital for their businesses, and experience 3.5 times faster growth than those without mentors. And in fact, of the companies surveyed, few managed to scale a profitable business model without a mentor's aid.

Even Steve Jobs, the famously visionary and dictatorial founder of Apple, relied on mentors, such as former football coach and Intuit CEO Bill Campbell, to keep himself sharp.

So, data indicates that those who train with successful people who've "been there" tend to achieve success faster. The winning formula, it seems, is to seek out the world's best and convince them to coach us.

Except there's one small wrinkle. That's not quite true.

We just held up Justin Bieber as an example of great, rapid-mentorship success. But since his rapid rise, he's gotten into an increasing amount of trouble. Fights. DUIs. Resisting arrest. Drugs. At least one story about egging someone's house. It appears that Bieber started unraveling nearly as quickly as he rocketed to *Billboard* number one.

OK, first of all, Bieber's young. He's acting like the rock star he is. But his mentor, Usher, also got to *Billboard* number one at age 18, and *he* managed to dominate pop music for a decade without DUIs or egg-vandalism incidents. Could it be that Bieber missed something in the mentorship process?

History, it turns out, is full of people who've been lucky enough to have amazing mentors and have stumbled anyway.

Indeed, equal amounts of research support both assertions:

that mentorship works *and* that it doesn't. Mentoring programs break down in the workplace so often that scholarly research contradicts itself about the value of mentoring at all, and prompts *Harvard Business Review* articles with titles such as "Why Mentoring Doesn't Work."

The mentorship slip is illustrated well by family businesses: 70 percent of them fail when passed to the second generation. A business-owner parent is in a perfect spot to mentor his or her child to run a company. And yet, sometime between mentorship and the business handoff, something critical doesn't stick.

One of the most tantalizing ideas about training with a master is that the master can help her protégé skip several steps up the ladder. Sometimes this ends up producing Aristotle. But sometimes it produces Icarus, to whom his father and master craftsman Daedalus of Greek mythology gave wings; Icarus then flew too high too fast and died.

Jimmy Fallon's mentor, one of the best-connected managers Jimmy could have for his *SNL* dream, served him up on a platter to *SNL* auditions in a fraction of the expected time it should take a new comedian to get there. But Jimmy didn't cut it—yet.

There was still one more ingredient, the one that makes the difference between rapid-rising protégés who soar and those who melt their wings and crash.

III.

In the mid-1990s, local outrage bubbled over some distressing news at Great Ormond Street Hospital (GOSH), a children's clinic in London: The beloved 150-year-old medical facility, to which J. M. Barrie had bequeathed the rights to his play *Peter Pan* in 1929, was killing children.

Not on purpose, of course. But a perplexingly high mortality rate plagued the facility's cardiac ward. Doctors studied the hospital's surgery processes and determined that a large number of fatalities occurred due to problems during the handovers between the operating room and the intensive care unit.

The risks of opening up a tiny child's chest cavity and repairing her heart are already terrifyingly high. But once she's stitched up, the medical staff must transfer all her life support equipment—monitoring lines, ventilator, vasodilators—not once, but twice: first, between the OR and a wheeled bed for transport, then again to a bed in the ICU. The process typically takes about 15 minutes. There were plenty of opportunities to screw up during the shuffle, but especially worrisome was the knowledge transfer. When the nuances of each particular case that were learned in surgery were lost in the handovers, patients suffered.

For years, the medical staff, exhausted after marathon surgeries, simply tried to *do better* at handovers. Nobody wanted these kids to die. But not only did errors persist, 30 percent of handover-related problems were caused by both equipment and information errors—the staff doubly screwed up.

One day, after lengthy surgeries, two tired doctors, Martin Elliott and Alan Goldman, sat down in front of a television for a break. Unbeknownst to them, that short break would change everything for the hospital.

"I'd done a transplant, then an arterial switch in the morning, and we were both pretty knackered," said Elliott. "The Formula 1 came on TV just as we were sitting down."

The doctors watched the drivers zoom around a racetrack at 300 kilometers per hour. Then, one car pulled over to the side of the circuit for a pit stop, "and we just realized," Dr. Elliott said, "that the pit stop where they changed tires and topped up the fuel was pretty well identical in concept to what we do in handover."

In seven seconds, the pit crew tore off four tires, filled a tank of gas, screwed on four new tires, and leapt out of the way for the car to scream back onto the track. Working as if controlled by a hive mind, the Formula 1 crews made the GOSH staff look like monkeys fighting over ventilator tubes.

"So we phoned them up."

Before long, the GOSH doctors found themselves hanging out with a Ferrari pit team in Italy. The mechanics demonstrated their process for the doctors up close and in detail.

Right away the GOSH team observed several differences between the Ferrari routine and their own. The pit crew meticulously planned out every possible scenario of what could go wrong during a handover and practiced each scenario until it became habit; GOSH staff, on the other hand, handled surprises on the fly.

Ferrari crewmembers operated with lots of physical space between each other; the hospital staff constantly got in each other's way—by virtue of the small space, they claimed. But a dozen grown men with power tools managed to gather round about as small a space during every race without bottlenecking anybody.

Ferrari pit crews had a dedicated overseer who ran the show. This overseer, often called a "lollipop man," would stand back to watch and direct the operation holistically. Only when he waved his flag would the car be allowed back onto the track. In a hospital room full of surgeons, anesthesiologists, and nurses, there was no conductor, no lollipop man. Each staff member simply helped out where he or she thought help was needed.

Finally, the GOSH doctors noted that the Ferrari technicians worked in silence. In contrast, hospital handovers were full of chatter; they not only talked through what was happening ("Ventilator is reattached!") but just *chatted* during the procedure.

When the doctors returned to London, they hired a dance choreographer to practice movements and add space to the small working area around a hospital bed. They turned the handover scramble into a routine, where each staffer had a prescribed set of actions. Contingencies for various scenarios were mapped out, then practiced. The head anesthesiologist became the lollipop man, standing back to observe and direct.

And everyone shut up.

Before long, the hospital had reduced its worst handover errors by 66 percent.

AFTER TRAINING WITH MASTER handover artists, the GOSH team created a life-saving shift at the hospital. The Formula 1 mentorship clearly worked out for them, and probably better than if the doctors had asked handover experts from another hospital for help.

But what about the training made it work, especially when so many other mentorship relationships don't?

The answer comes from the research of a young psychologist named Christina M. Underhill, who in the early 2000s noticed something troubling. Like most of us, she'd grown up with *Star Wars* and other heroes-with-mentors storylines. But when she dug into the academic side of mentorship, she observed that most studies were either scientifically unsound, or produced contradictory results. Common wisdom said that protégés benefited from being mentored by more experienced colleagues—just as we learn from the Greeks—but many of the reports she saw disagreed on not only *if* mentorship worked, but how well, and under what circumstances.

Underhill compiled 25 years of mentorship research—more than 100 studies—and looked at the data. She tossed out flawed case studies and anecdotal articles marketing particular coaching programs, and focused on research in which the career outcomes of mentees at work were measured and compared with the outcomes of those who were not mentored.

The statistics showed that businesspeople who were mentored in the workplace tended to achieve slightly more at work, on average, than those who didn't. Counterintuitively, however, "Informal mentoring," Underhill found, "produced a larger and more significant effect on career outcomes than formal mentoring."

The mentorship study data conflicted, it turned out, because of the difference between structured mentoring programs, which were less effective, and mentorship that happened organically. In fact, one-on-one mentoring in which an organization formally matched people proved to be nearly as worthless as a person having not been mentored at all. However, when students and mentors came together on their own and formed personal relationships, the mentored did significantly better, as measured by future income, tenure, number of promotions, job satisfaction, work stress, and self-esteem.

This is why Sheryl Sandberg, the COO of Facebook and the author of *Lean In*, dedicates a chapter in her book to this concept, arguing that asking someone to formally mentor you is like asking a celebrity for an autograph; it's stiff, inorganic, and often doesn't work out. "Searching for a mentor has become the professional equivalent of waiting for Prince Charming," she writes. "Young women are told that if they can just find the right mentor, they will be pushed up the ladder and whisked away to the corner office to live happily ever after. Once again, we are teaching women to be too dependent on others." This waiting for luck to strike is the antithesis of lateral thinking. And the research shows she's right.

All those expensive mentorship programs that corporations put on to smash strangers together in the hopes of increased success are basically just rolling dice. But in light of Underhill's research, the GOSH doctors did something very right: They managed to build an *organic* bond with the Formula 1 pit crews. By the time the handover problems had been fixed, the relationship between the doctors and racers had developed beyond what Elliott and Goldman originally envisioned. They had gone to Formula 1 seeking technical help, and ended up becoming friends.

The GOSH doctors and nurses needed to model moves of master handoverers, and nobody beat Formula 1 pit crews at complicated equipment swaps. Ferrari's process for tire replacement didn't map exactly to unhooking and rehooking ventilators, but its masterful approach to teamwork in tight spaces did. And the Ferrari team was delighted to coach the doctors.

That solved the short-term problem. But long-term success of the hospital was accelerated by the *deep relationship*. Over the next several years, the Formula 1 made GOSH its official charity, raising more than £3 million for the children and hosting events where sick kids and their parents could hang out with the racing stars and for a moment forget their pain. The racers became invested in the success of Great Ormond Street as a whole.

There's a big difference, in other words, between having a mentor guide our practice and having a mentor guide our journey.

OUR TYPICAL PARADIGM FOR mentorship is that of a young, enterprising worker sitting across from an elderly executive at an oak desk, engaging in Q&A about how to succeed at specific challenges.

On the other hand, a smartcut-savvy mentee approaches things a bit differently. She develops personal relationships with her mentors, asks their advice on other aspects of life, not just the formal challenge at hand. And she cares about her mentors' lives too.

Business owner Charlie Kim, founder of Next Jump and one of my own mentors, calls this vulnerability. It's the key, he says, to developing a deep and organic relationship that leads to journey-focused mentorship and not just a focus on practice. Both the teacher and the student must be able to open up about their fears, and that builds trust, which in turn accelerates learning. That trust opens us up to actually heeding the difficult advice we might otherwise ignore. "It drives you to do more," Kim says. The best mentors help students to realize that the things that really matter are not the big and obvious. The more vulnerability is shown in the relationship, the more critical details become available for a student to pick up on, and assimilate.

And, crucially, a mentor with whom we have that kind of relationship will be more likely to tell us "no" when we need it—and we'll be more likely to listen.

IV.

The troubling thing about all these mentorship stories so far is they seem to depend heavily on luck. Chess prodigy Josh Waitzkin didn't seek out a master to train him; one found him in the park. Justin Bieber was randomly discovered by his manager-to-be via YouTube. Telemachus was fortuitously visited by a *goddess*. The busy Ferrari team were willing to meet with the GOSH doctors in the first place.

Aristotle was privileged to study at Plato's Academy, but some kid on the other side of the world was probably just as promising as young Aristotle and never got the mentorship.

How can building deep relationships with master mentors be a smartcut if it hinges on our being lucky enough to know the master?

Hip-hop icon Jay-Z gives us a clue in one of his lyrics, "We were kids without fathers . . . so we found our fathers on wax and on the streets and in history. We got to pick and choose the ancestors who would inspire the world we were going to make for ourselves."

In ancient Greece, few people had access to the best mentors. Jay-Z didn't either, but he had books from which he could get an inkling about what those kinds of mentors were like. With every increase in communication, with every autobiography published, and every YouTube video of a superstar created, we increase our access to the great models in every category. This allows us to at least study the moves that make masters great—which is a start.

Some people are naturally good at making this work. Sam Walton, founder of Walmart, studied and stole moves from master retailers fabulously well. He openly admitted it. "Most everything I've done, I've copied from someone else," he said.

The problem is that two people can study the same business model, watch the same video, or even take the same advice from a mentor, and one person might pick up critical details that the other misses. The late literary giant Saul Bellow would call someone with the ability to spot important details among noise a "first-class noticer." *This is a key difference between those who learn more quickly than others.*

Jack Canfield, who we met earlier, explains that though mastery of those details can come from "modeling [the master], whether conscious or unconscious: their thinking, their visualizing, their body posture, their breathing patterns," the benefit of an in-person relationship is that the mentor can help the student focus on the most important elements. "A master is able to give you feedback on a much more nuanced level, [and] has very little patience with distraction."

The reason GOSH and Telemachus and the other successful mentees in this chapter succeeded in the long run is that mentors who were invested in their success, who showed vulnerability and cared enough to tell them what they didn't want to hear when they needed to hear it, forced them to examine success-crucial details *more closely than they might have on their own.*

Which brings us back to that troubling question. How do people accelerate success when they don't have personal access to great mentors, when they can do nothing but watch their videos and read their biographies? Especially when first-class noticing doesn't come naturally?

It turns out that the answer is exactly how young Jimmy Fallon got his break.

V.

When the *SNL* people called Jimmy Fallon in 1998 to audition for a newly opened slot in the cast, they said, "No Troll doll."

Two years had passed since Jimmy's first attempt to get on *Saturday Night Live*. In the meantime, he'd practiced nonstop. Siegel had arranged a relentless schedule of stand-up performances in front of audiences who she knew in many cases would decimate him. It toughened him up. She made him rehearse his voice impressions with his back turned; if she couldn't recognize Jimmy's characters with her eyes closed, she cut them from the act. Like Mr. Miyagi from *The Karate Kid*, Siegel taught her young charge confidence and attention to detail. By that time, Jimmy was no longer simply Siegel's client; he had become a dear friend.

Short-term job opportunities came and went as Jimmy built credibility in the L.A. comedy scene; Siegel cared more about his long-term journey than his short-term paycheck; she screened every offer through the lens of, "Will this help Jimmy get *SNL* one day?" He said "no" to television sitcoms, "no" to acting jobs that might take him too far away from *SNL*. When Jimmy booked stand-up gigs in New York, Siegel phoned *SNL* people to check out his progress.

During those two years, agents turned their backs on Jimmy, and hungry managers whispered in his ear, saying if he ditched Siegel, he'd be better off. But Siegel believed in Jimmy's fanatical dream as much as he did, and Jimmy preferred to work hard with someone like her, as opposed to an old-school manager to whom Jimmy would be just one of many small bets.

And so, at age 23, Jimmy Fallon found himself once again on stage in front of Lorne Michaels. Still young and fresh-faced, but more polished and a little less terrified of the gray-haired king of comedy sitting in front of him, Jimmy was after a small win this time: not a spot in the cast, but just to make Michaels laugh.

This time, unlike many other auditioners who showcased mainly celebrity impersonations, Jimmy impersonated a bevy of other *comedians*: Chris Rock, Gilbert Gottfried, Bill Cosby, Colin Quinn. His impressions were dead-on. When he spoke in these great comedians' voices, he *became* them.

Then, his lifelong obsession with Adam Sandler suddenly paid off. Jimmy later recalled, "After about 3 bits, I did the Adam Sandler bit, and Lorne Michaels laughed."

"And then I blacked out."

JIMMY WAS TALENTED AND funny, but so are a lot of people who try out for *SNL*. However, Jimmy's routine, the one where he stole the voices of master comedians, stood out to Michaels and the rest of the crew. *If this guy can become these funny people so vividly, he can be funny on our show.*

They hired him. Jimmy's dream had come true.

Jimmy Fallon got *SNL* not just because he had a great relationship with a great manager, but because of another deep relationship: the one he'd spent his entire life developing with comedians he hadn't met. From a young age, he'd studied their videos obsessively, learned everything about their lives and what they were like. When Siegel called him that first time, Jimmy already knew who she was; he'd memorized her name and myriad more facts about his long-distance "mentor," Adam Sandler. Jimmy's intimate connection with these comedians drove him to master the tiny details that would separate his performance from aspiring comics who moved on once their celebrity impressions were "good enough."

As we've learned, mentorship doesn't always yield success. But when we look at superlative success stories throughout history, the presence of an in-person mentor (in Jimmy's case his manager) or a world-class, long-distance mentor (in Jimmy's case, great comedians whom he copied) with whom the mentee has a deep, vulnerable relationship is almost always manifest. The smartcut is the same:

The world's youngest Nobel Prize winner, 25-year-old Lawrence Bragg, won the coveted award for physics in 1915 in conjunction with his father, master physicist William Bragg, who had mentored his son in the lab. (The younger Bragg, who was later knighted, went on to run the lab where James Watson and Francis Crick discovered DNA.)

The billion-dollar micro-blogging service Tumblr earned its founder, 26-year-old David Karp, $200 million in 2013, after six years of hard work. But it was in the second year that everything changed; that was when Karp brought in his personal mentor and friend, tech executive John Maloney, to guide him and the Tumblr rocket ship to maturity. This story is a repeat of that of countless other fast-growing companies.

And comedian Louis C.K., who as we saw earlier did things the hard way for 15 years, finally transformed his career with this same smartcut. In his depression as a failing comic, C.K. turned to his childhood comic icon, George Carlin. He resolved to tick like Carlin ticked. So he started to mimic Carlin's process, memorize the details of his life. He soaked in Carlin's style of telling raw, honest stories about himself—jokes that exposed Carlin's human vulnerabilities—and began telling similarly vulnerable jokes about himself.

When C.K.'s long-distance connection with Carlin became more than mimicry, it transformed him. And that's when his career finally took off.

You can feel the depth of that relationship when C.K. speaks about Carlin. "He was a beacon for me," C.K. said, choking with emotion, to a crowd at the New York Public Library in 2010, after Carlin's passing. "I'm doing exactly what he taught me to do."

AFTER MICHAELS TOLD JIMMY he'd made *SNL*, Jimmy and Siegel went out for a celebratory dinner. They picked a fancy spot, called a friend, and ordered manhattans at the bar, in honor of Jimmy's soon-to-be home. The restaurant staff brought out a cake and candle in Jimmy's honor.

He blew out the candle.

And then he got suddenly quiet.

"What's wrong?" Siegel asked.

"Since I can remember," Jimmy said, "whenever I blew out candles, I wished for *Saturday Night Live*."

For the first time in his life, he didn't know what to wish for.

Chapter 3

RAPID FEEDBACK

"The F Word"

I.

The most popular post on Eli Pariser's blog on the day after he launched it was about Gandhi. Twelve people shared it.

The post told the story of the talisman the revered Indian leader once gave to his grandson Arun, which listed the seven "blunders" he believed led to violence:

> *Wealth without work.*
> *Pleasure without conscience.*
> *Knowledge without character.*
> *Commerce without morality.*
> *Science without humanity.*
> *Religion without sacrifice.*
> *Politics without principle.*

Number six on the list soon became the most poignant; on his way to a prayer meeting shortly after he gave Arun the note, Mahatma Gandhi was assassinated.

The same day that Pariser posted the Gandhi story on his blog, the top story on the hugely popular blog *BuzzFeed* was "20

Supporting Characters from '90s TV Shows Then and Now"—a collection of embarrassing before-and-after pictures of goofy stars from shows like *Clarissa Explains It All* and *Even Stevens*.

That post was shared by 30,000 people. It reached 800,000 viewers.

This was the very phenomenon that drove Pariser, a mellow, unshaven author and activist from Maine, to start his blog: As more people used social networks like Facebook, the speed at which content—stories, videos, pictures—could spread to huge audiences, or "go viral," was increasing. And yet what spread farthest seemed to be the inane stuff of tabloids. Sex tapes and home videos of people injuring themselves. Cat photos and celebrity wardrobe malfunctions. The most popular stuff on the Web was at best benignly entertaining, at worst degrading.

And yet, there was so much important content out there, Pariser noted, that wasn't getting any attention at all. People were missing the diverse cultural perspectives and heartwarming stories the Internet could now deliver faster than ever. *What if there was a way to make the good stuff go viral?* Pariser mused.

So he recruited a friend, Peter Koechley, an editor from a humor publication called *The Onion*, to help him do just that. They would find righteous but overlooked content and package it in ways that made it more "shareable." This mostly meant taking good stories with boring headlines from obscure parts of the Internet and writing clever—and potentially more viral—headlines, then republishing those stories on their own blog, with credit and links back to the original.

They quit their jobs, launched the blog, and started a Facebook page to promote it. They parlayed Pariser's credibility as a successful author in order to talk a few investors, including Facebook cofounder Chris Hughes and Reddit cofounder Alexis Ohanian, into giving them enough money to operate a shoestring staff.

They called it all *Upworthy*. Mission: "To make important stuff as viral as a video of some idiot surfing off his roof."

Emboldened and idealistic, *Upworthy* combed the Internet, gathering stories of ordinary people fighting inequality, veterans giving inspiring speeches, and do-gooders generally doing good. *Upworthy* gave these stories alluring headlines and catchy thumbnails and provocative commentary, then pushed them back out. About five times a day.

And hardly anyone noticed.

Media companies typically take years to build; audiences gather over time, after a publisher gains trust through consistency. Even in the fast-paced Internet era where technology made it possible to launch a blog in minutes, *BuzzFeed*, *The Huffington Post*, and other popular blogs had only grown to reach mass audiences after five or more years of hard work. And that was fast, compared to newspapers and magazines of earlier eras.

Upworthy had cash for a few months, in which time it needed to either convince investors to put in more money, or start turning a profit. Each day, *Upworthy* stories rolled out—three shares here, 25 there.

Meanwhile, the week after *Upworthy* launched, *BuzzFeed* published an article entitled "33 Animals Who Are Extremely Disappointed in You," which received over 2 million views.

While the clock ticked away and *Upworthy*'s bank account slowly shrank, the adorable baby meerkats (#28) seemed to be sneering at Pariser.

"TELL ME, DO YOU think this man is dorky, Jewish, or autistic?"

I sat in a low-ceilinged comedy cellar on the third floor of a building on the North Side of Chicago, while three girls on the stage in front of me pretended to be contestants in some sort of vaguely anti-Semitic game show. In response to the question, which floated in the open for a moment while I bit my tongue, a spectacled twenty-something boy with a pinched voice leapt onto the stage.

"I'm dorky, Jewish, *and* autistic!" he announced to the girls, triumphantly. Then, after a brief pause, he delivered what was apparently the punch line. "Boom!"

No one in the small theater made a sound. We just sat. Trying to decide if we should be offended or feel sorry.

In the back of the room, a woman with thick-rimmed glasses grimaced. For a few long seconds, the awkwardness hung in the air. Finally, the woman with glasses mercifully shouted, "Scene!"

This was the worst live comedy performance I'd ever seen. The performers had another hour to go.

Ugh.

The little comedy theater belonged to The Second City, the world-renowned humor academy that NPR once called "the Harvard of ha-ha." As a guest of the executive director, Kelly Leonard, a veteran comedyman who had trained stars like Stephen Colbert, I was shadowing a class of ten students who were preparing to graduate from comedy school. After two years of training, they were practicing for their final show, in which they would perform *Saturday Night Live*–style skits for a packed crowd, in four weeks.

Founded in 1959, The Second City has been the training ground for some of the most well-known comedians on the planet, from ghostbuster Dan Aykroyd to *Parks and Recreation* star Amy Poehler. The school is known for pioneering a style of comedy called improv, a blend of pantomime, character impersonations, and impromptu dialogue. It's a zany, difficult art. This group of actors seemed to be terrible at it.

A few of them had acting talent. One woman excelled at character voices, another at funny facial expressions. A young man named Calvin did an uncanny Barack Obama. But as the students climbed on and off the stage to perform scenes they'd written, the output wasn't just unfunny, it was depressing.

They made fun of handicapped kids. They acted out awkward romances. One kid put a backpack under his shirt, but had to explain that he was impersonating an obese football coach when nobody got his joke. Then, without explanation, two students spent several minutes pantomiming the folding of a large number of imaginary shirts.

It was a train wreck. But without the mercy of a swift death.

This was supposed to be the best comedy school in the world. These kids had to audition to be here. Giants like Steve Carell and Tina Fey studied here just a few years ago. In fact, it was not long after taking this very class that Fey landed a career-making writing job at *SNL*.

How could they be about to *graduate*? After 50 years, was the revered Second City simply going downhill?

No, Leonard assured me. *These kids are on to something.* In fact, I'd soon learn that this terrible comedy was the root of a smartcut that had transformed businesses across the globe, as well as the careers of many a budding entertainer.

To fully understand just what that something was, and how through the same method *Upworthy* might get people to care more about do-gooding than mocking celebrities, we're going to have to talk a little about death. . . .

II.

On a September evening in New York City, several dozen twenty- and thirty-somethings filed into chairs at 412 Broadway for a wake. A bagpiper played "Amazing Grace."

The screeching sound filled the narrow, dimly lit room. A man in a pastor's garb and a clerical collar stood at the front, welcoming people. He was backlit by a large projector screen.

As the crowd settled in and the bagpipes faded out, the pastor spoke. "My name is Leo," he boomed. "Welcome to Startup Funeral."

The dearly departed that evening consisted of three defunct tech companies. Unlike most funerals, this one was sponsored by various liquor companies and bore the slogan, "Putting the Fun in Funeral."

"Startups are afraid to talk to people about what went wrong," Pastor Leo continued. "If you don't learn anything, appreciate the fact that these people are brave enough to come up and talk."

One by one, executives from the three companies took the microphone, recounting the demise of the companies to which they had dedicated months or years. Brian, cofounder of Addieu, an iPhone application that helped people connect over social networks when there was no phone signal, explained why no one downloaded his app: "It was not easy to spell. It's a French word that we added a letter to." But more important, he recognized, at the end of the day he'd "built something that nobody wanted." After about six months, he shut the app down.

Brian was followed by Dan, CEO of Get-A-Game, a service that helped people find local sports activities. He lamented the slow death of the business. "I thought it was a good idea . . . in the end, we ran out of funds."

The most depressing eulogy was Chris's. The former chief technical officer of Kozmo.com, a delivery site that would take anything you ordered online and deliver it to your door in an hour, explained how his company went from six people in a basement to 300 people in a five-floor office with $280 million from investors. In the heyday of the early Web, the company spared no expense to advertise its services everywhere: billboards, TV commercials, and countless Internet ads. "We were losing money with every order," Chris said. "But the 'gray hairs' in the room said we needed to cut corporate costs instead . . . there was no plan." In a couple of years, the company had burned most of its investors' cash and slowly laid everyone off.

The beer-filled techie crowd laughed at parts, muttered "ouch" at others. By the end, the funeral felt like—perhaps fittingly—a strange mix of celebration and group therapy.

"We hope your future endeavors are not as bad as your first ones," Pastor Leo said in closing.

Then the bagpipes started, and everyone got drunk.

Oscar Wilde once said, "Experience is the name everyone gives to their mistakes." The mourners at Startup Funeral are among the many people in the American technology culture who regularly celebrate said experience. Since the rise of the Web, the Silicon Valley crowd has decided that failure in the quest to build a business is not only OK, but *cool*. "Fail often" is a guiding aphorism.

Research shows that Americans, in general, are more tolerant of business failure than people in any other country. They don't have a higher *rate* of business success, but the low social consequences for failing make risks easier to justify, and therefore many people take them. Contrast this with many other parts of the world, where entrepreneurs and their families often face huge social stigma for having started a business and failed. In Japan, for example, a bankrupt business will often ruin its founder. "Here you only get one chance," Japanese entrepreneur Kazuo Honda told the *Financial Times* in 2011. "People don't try if they think they might fail." Historically, failed businessmen were often ostracized in their communities, making it difficult to find work later, or committed suicide. This proved a huge disincentive to taking the risk of starting a business in the first place.

"This is an innate issue for humans and one we have to

overcome," says Dr. Bradley Staats, who teaches business at the University of North Carolina, Chapel Hill. Obviously, in some settings, failure can be catastrophic if we don't do things right the first time (for example, landing on an aircraft carrier or building a nuclear power plant), he says. But with many things, the actual, long-term consequences of failure are negligible.

Anyone who's started a business, gotten a great job, won political office, or invented something did so in the face of risk. Yet our survival instinct is to minimize the likelihood of bad things happening to us. In business, the more socially acceptable it is to fail, the more likely smart people will try crazy things, the geeks argue.

"If you're not failing you are either very lucky, very good, or not pushing the boundaries enough," Staats says. Fortunately, as startup culture spreads, and the Facebook generation grows up, the global social stigma around starting a business and failing— and failure in general—has decreased. This destigmatization actually makes failure less risky.

Wonderful news! Let's all try crazy things and fail! Not so fast . . .

In 2008 four Harvard researchers looked at historical data of people who started businesses in America between 1975 and 2003. Their goal was to see how well founders who'd previously failed in business did with subsequent businesses. Had they learned from their past failures? They compared the failures to founders who'd successfully taken a company public, and entrepreneurs who'd never started a business before.

It turns out that after you adjust for statistical margin of error, an entrepreneur who'd failed in a previous venture was not likely to do better than someone who'd never run a business in her life. Expecting to be suddenly great at business after running one into the ground is akin to losing the first basketball game you ever played and expecting to win the next game *because* you lost the first one.

According to the study, successful entrepreneurs, on the other hand, are 50 percent more likely to succeed in a second venture. The more you win, the more likely you are to win again.

This lines up with the results of a 2011 study of 3,200 early-stage technology companies by Startup Compass. "For software companies with very high market risk," explains researcher Bjoern Herrmann, "the uncertainty is so overwhelming that the experience that you have from a previous company doesn't seem to have a significant impact on the actual success of a [second] company."

Whereas the entrepreneurs who eulogized their companies at Startup Funeral may have been doing their part in a needed effort to get people more comfortable with taking risks, each founder himself was actually hardly a better bet for a future investor than he was when he started Kozmo or Get-A-Game or whatever that other one was called.

So, failing in business doesn't make us better or smarter. But succeeding makes us more likely to continue to succeed. This, of course, poses a chicken-and-egg problem. How do we increase the chance of success if the best way to do so is to . . . already . . . succeed?

All great successes make mistakes along the way. NBA star Michael Jordan missed more than 9,000 shots and lost 300 games in his career. He was the best, and he failed *a lot*.

And yet, it looks like the advice of "what doesn't kill you makes you stronger" and "failure makes you wiser" isn't actually true.

III.

In the United States, one-third of hospital patient volume and one-third of Medicare spending goes to cardiac care.

As our hearts beat, a small portion of the oxygen they process gets pushed through the coronary arteries, small tubes that supply O_2 directly to the heart muscle itself. It's a brilliant perpetual motion machine, like a battery that powers its own charger. But as we age, plaque builds up inside the coronary artery, making it harder and harder for enough blood to squeeze through. This leads to heart attacks and is caused by cheeseburgers.

Surgeons resolve the plaque problem by installing new tubes in bad hearts to bypass the clogged sections—essentially rerouting blood through a new hose. This is called coronary artery bypass grafting, or CABG. It's a tricky procedure that requires stopping the patient's heart, quickly attaching the new tube, then jump-starting the heart back to life.

Of course, our hearts don't come with on/off switches for a reason. Stopping them, even for a moment, can cause permanent damage, especially to the brain. An unfortunate number of CABG surgery patients end up having strokes or suffering mental disorders after the procedure.*

In the late '90s, however, researchers figured out a way to do CABG without stopping the heart. This meant surgeons who'd been performing the surgery for decades had to learn a new procedure, which required more dexterity. With it, more lives would be saved, and side effects spared.

This change excited Bradley Staats (whom we met earlier in this chapter), who was then a researcher at Harvard Business School. Not because he was expecting heart surgery anytime soon, but because he was conducting research on failure, and suddenly a whole lot of surgeons were about to fail, despite a life-or-death motivation not to.

For ten years, Staats and his associates followed surgeons

---

* Some studies have indicated that as many as 50 percent of patients had some sort of cognitive decline after the surgery.

as they learned to do CABG on beating hearts. Staats observed a total of 6,516 operations and tracked the mortality rates of patients from surgeon to surgeon—adjusted for factors like age and health. He studied how the surgeons learned to get the procedure right, and what happened when they didn't. By the time the researchers published their results, Staats had become a professor at UNC and a slew of patients had lived to eat more cheeseburgers.

But along the way, a number of surgeries by the transitioning doctors ended in failure. Staats and his colleagues combed through the data from all the surgeries, looking for patterns: How did a surgeon's failure in one operation affect future surgeries? How quickly did doctors learn, and did failure help them improve?

They called the results a "paradox of failure."

It turns out that the surgeons who botched the new procedure tended to do worse in subsequent surgeries. Rather than learning from their mistakes, their success rates continuously declined. On the other hand, when surgeons did well on the new surgery, more successes tended to follow. Just like the startups in the Compass and Harvard studies.

But what's really interesting is what happened to the surgeons who saw *their colleagues* fail at the new CABG procedure. These showed significant increases in their own success rates with every failure that they saw another doctor experience. Further perplexing, however: seeing a colleague perform a successful surgery didn't seem to translate to one's own future success.

It was indeed a paradox. Screwups got worse. When colleagues screwed up, observers got better. When a doctor succeeded, she did better on her subsequent surgeries. When her colleagues did well, it didn't affect her.

There's no fun in the funeral of a heart patient whose surgery you failed. But every doctor fails sometimes. Seasoned physicians learn to become mentally and emotionally immune to it. They learn to live with the reality that some patients don't survive.

Staats concluded that this coping mechanism was itself responsible for the paradox. He and his colleagues called this attribution theory. The theory says that people explain their successes and failures "by attributing them to factors that will allow them to feel as good as possible about themselves."

Remember what the Startup Funeral founders said?

"We ran out of money."

"People didn't want it."

"The 'gray hairs' had no plan."

Look at what they did. They each attributed their companies' failures to *external* factors. Things that made them feel better about *themselves*.

Think back to the last time you lost a competition, or your favorite sports team lost a game. Did you blame the weather or the referees? Or perhaps player injuries or a lucky roll of the dice? If you did—or were tempted to—you're normal. We're wired to think this way.

On the other hand, we tend to pin our successes on internal factors. Think back to the last competition *you* won. It was your hard work, your skill, your quick thinking in the heat of the moment that won the day. Right?

This is exactly what the heart surgeons did. When they failed at the CABG, it was because of bad luck. It was hard to see. The patient was unstable. There wasn't enough time.

"When interpreting their own failures," Staats explains, "individuals tend to make external attributions, pointing to factors that are outside of their direct control, such as luck. As a result, their motivation to exert effort on the same task in the future is reduced."

Interesting. When doctors failed due to what they perceived as bad luck, they didn't tend to work any smarter the next time. They attributed failure in a way that made them feel as good as they could about themselves.

"Even though an individual failure experience may contain valuable knowledge," Staats says, "without subsequent effort to reflect upon that experience, the potential learning will remain untapped.

"Further, since individuals tend to seek knowledge about themselves in ways designed to yield flattering results, even if someone were to engage in reflection after failing, he might seek knowledge to *explain away the failure*." (Emphasis mine.)

This is a survival mechanism. We externalize our mistakes because we need to live with ourselves afterward.

We have no problem assuming responsibility for our successes, though, even if we don't brag about them. Staats explains, "People tend to attribute their own success to their effort and ability. Since they have control over their own effort and actions, these attributions motivate them to exert effort in subsequent tasks so that they can continue improving and learning." This made the successful doctors better and better.

However, when failure isn't personal, we often do the opposite. When someone else fails, we blame his or her lack of effort or ability. When we see people succeed, we tend to attribute it to situational forces beyond their control, namely luck.

For the cardiac surgeons, this made the failure of a colleague quite valuable. Since it was *that guy's* fault, fellow surgeons instinctually zeroed in on the mistakes. "I'll make sure not to do that," they said subconsciously. And they got better at the surgery.

And that's what, if you've stayed with me this long, brings us back to those terrible comedians at The Second City.

IV.

It had been five hours since the Jewish autism joke and my chest hurt.

Please make them stop, I thought. *I can't breathe.*

I was sitting along the railing of the second level of the Mainstage Theater, just one floor down from the comedy cellar I'd visited earlier that day. The spotlights shone on the red curtain at the back of the stage, an armada of lights and cameras hung from the ceiling. In front of the curtains, a Second City troupe bounced around, wearing tailored suits and fancy dresses and nerdy glasses, performing a 90-minute sketch and musical comedy show called *Let Them Eat Chaos.*

And chaos it was. The audience howled with delight as a lovely actress sang a song about whales while her coactor suddenly sprayed water from his mouth. A gangly man and a short, blond woman put on Castilian accents and recited hilarious rhymes, generating streams of guffaw-fueled tears from the front rows. When two of the actors performed a rap song about Pinkberry frozen yogurt, I thought the cackling 60-year-old woman next to me was going to need CABG surgery.

This was proper comedy. As the comedians scampered about the stage, delivering hilarious one-liners and memorable scenes, I couldn't help but ask myself:

How long had these guys been at this?

As I soon discovered, the answer was "barely longer than the students you watched." But how could that be? The evening show had people falling out of their seats, wiping tears. The students had me wanting to cry for other reasons.

The secret—The Second City's hack—one learns, is in what happens each evening after the show. Every night, once the curtains close, the cast comes back out on stage. *The show's over*, but the audience can stick around if it likes, while the cast practices improv. *We haven't rehearsed this*, they say. *But we promise to try to keep you laughing.* Of course, most of the audience usually stays.

In this second performance, things subtly shift. The language changes; the actors' approach becomes more casual. It's late at night, and it's free. So the expectation is set that, as Kelly Leonard tells me, "It may suck, and that's okay."

The after-hours set is still quite funny. But the pressure for the performers to give the audience its money's worth evaporates. They've already done that. And in this safe environment, the cast tests out new material.

And just like the students I watched, they bomb quite frequently.

The fast-paced improv format allows actors to redirect the action, change scenes, and cut off jokes that aren't working. Performers typically take audience suggestions for topics or backstories for characters, then act out the first thing that comes to mind. Amid all the zaniness that ensues, casts can slip in scenes they've been considering for their show and gauge audience reactions. And though sometimes the material is dreadful, it doesn't matter. They can fail without failing.

SINCE THE EARLY 20TH century, psychologists have argued about the effects of feedback interventions, or critiques, on behavior and performance. Various studies have shown that such interventions improved learning, while others "prove" that feedback has negative effects on performance. For years, academics debated whether positive feedback ("You're doing great!") was more helpful than negative feedback ("You did that wrong!"), and argued about whether direct, drill-sergeant–like feedback was more helpful than kind, tactful feedback. Results were all over the map. Everything worked sometimes, and everything didn't work sometimes.

Then in 1996, researchers Avraham N. Kluger and Angelo DeNisi looked at a hundred years of these studies and found something interesting: cumulatively, most feedback interventions were indeed not actually helpful to bettering performance, and much feedback indeed made things worse; however, some feedback was *very* helpful to boosting performance, and it had nothing to do with bedside manner.

The difference was how much the feedback caused a person to focus on himself rather than the task.

If you've ever been bowling, you may have experienced this effect (or seen someone else experience it). Everyone loves to give bowling advice to the guy who's losing. "Try throwing it harder," your friend says after you manage to knock down three pins. "Twist your wrist a little as you let go," says the girl who just bowled a strike, after you hit one more pin. The next time you're up, someone else says, "Aim just to the right of the middle pin," and the first guy adds, "Bend your knees." Your teammate reminds you, "You need to get a spare for us to still have a chance to win." So, you step up to the line and throw the ball—knees bent, wrist twisted, eyes staring to the right of the middle pin, and *what else am I supposed to be doing?!*—right into the gutter.

All that feedback made you worse at bowling. Not because it wasn't decent advice, but because a high-pressure feedback barrage tends to make us self-conscious. We get stuck inside our own heads. Kluger and DeNisi found that, as with bowling anxiety, the closer feedback moves our attention to ourselves, the worse it is for us.

The research showed that experts—people who were masters at a trade—vastly preferred negative feedback to positive. It spurred the most improvement. That was because criticism is generally more actionable than compliments. "You did well" is less helpful in improving your bowling game than "You turned your wrist too much."

Crucially, experts tended to be able to turn off the part of their egos that took legitimate feedback personally when it came to their craft, and they were confident enough to parse helpful feedback from incorrect feedback. Meanwhile novices psyched themselves out. They needed encouragement and feared failure.

The tough part about negative feedback is in separating ourselves from the perceived failure and turning our experiences into objective experiments. But when we do that, feedback becomes much more powerful.

This is how The Second City pumps out comedic talent so quickly.

Tina Fey, Seth Meyers, and the other famous comedians to come out of The Second City all bombed as badly as my students did during their training—over and over again. *The Office* star Steve Carell once had an audience storm out of the theater on him for a joke gone too far. Political satirist Stephen Colbert was begged off the stage one night when his bit about dial-up Internet nearly put the audience to sleep.

The Second City teaches its students to take such things in stride, to become scientists who see audience reaction as commentary on the joke, not the jokester. To turn off the part of their brains that says "I fail" when they get negative feedback. And then the school has students continuously parlay up to harder audiences and harsher feedback as they grow more comfortable. This forces them to both toughen up and push creative boundaries.

With this process, The Second City transforms failure (something that implies finality) into simply feedback (something that can be used to improve). Hundreds of times a week.

The Silicon Valley mantra "fail often" actually has a second part to it. More often than not, Valley startups will say, "fail fast and fail often." This gets at the principle of rapid feedback. But failing implies a finality, a funeral, an amen. And according to The Second City, that's not necessary.

— — — — — —

THE SECOND CITY MANAGES to accomplish three things to accelerate its performers' growth: (1) it gives them rapid feedback; (2) it depersonalizes the feedback; and (3) it lowers the stakes and pressure, so students take risks that force them to improve.

For the first year, Leonard explains, The Second City's goal is to get students used to anticipating negative feedback and to get them out of their own heads. This is about building confidence and creating a "safe" environment in which it's OK to screw up. Then, second-year classes ratchet up the feedback, putting actors in a succession of situations where they will fail small in front of live crowds. It's one thing for your coactor or director to tell you a joke is funny, but it's entirely another to hear the pins drop when a live audience disagrees. Or conversely to hear wild cackling from the crowd at something that may have seemed like a bad idea on paper. Every laugh or lack thereof becomes a data point that the actors can use to better themselves.

By embracing all these tiny failures, there is no actual failure.*

In contrast, a typical acting class might spend an entire semester building up to a single performance. Students practice together in class, but they don't know if the audience will like their show until the final day. And if the audience hates it, there's nothing students can do.

If you think about it, that's how most businesses operate. When releasing a new product, a company will spend months, sometimes years, fine-tuning, building up to one critical moment: the launch. Then on launch day the product either is a success or a failure.

---

* On that note: core to the Second City improv training is a concept called "Yes, and." On stage, when an actor says something unfunny and another actor says "no" or allows him to fail, a scene instantly loses its humor. "Yes, and" says that no matter how ridiculous or terrible another actor's line, the other actor's job is to validate the premise and then to say "and . . . " and to twist it to something else. This converts failure into humor.

People buy it and the company makes a profit, or they don't and the product fails.

The Second City, on the other hand, puts its students on stage in front of live crowds every week. The class I sat in on wasn't just practicing for the big show in four weeks; they were practicing for the little live show they did every week, the one with a crowd that would give them feedback on their material-in-progress. That's how in just eight weeks—half a typical college semester—a class can put together a full-length sketch comedy show and it will be extremely funny. They know, because they got the feedback early, and often.

"Speed is an essential part of our game," Leonard explains. "The rapid feedback . . . it's non-stop."

Rapid feedback forces students to constantly write new material, to push boundaries—both as actors and in the jokes they tell. That's why so many of the students I observed had such repulsive jokes; they were exploring the "line" from a safe environment. "Sometimes I put things in to burn them," Anne, the teacher with the glasses, confessed to me before her class got on stage. She'll give the go-ahead on scenes she knows the audience will not laugh at, because her students don't become funnier by being prevented from taking risks.

"Funny is right at the line. Just a little bit uncomfortable. Just at the place where it could fail," she says. "And just like a muscle, you have to fail a little bit in order to improve."

"We do that to them over and over and over again."

V.

Not long ago, on a sleepy day in Stillwater, Minnesota, Zachary Sobiech, a cheerful, square-jawed 14-year-old boy learned he had osteosarcoma, a deadly cancer of the bones, and chances were slim that he would survive it.

In an instant, the Sobiech family's life turned upside down. Zach went to chemotherapy, but after apparently successful procedures, X-rays showed new tumors in his lungs. Zach decided to accept his fate and live what life he had left to the fullest. "You can either sit in your basement and wait," he said. "Or you can get out there and do some crazy stuff."

With thin, postchemo blond hair and a permanent smile, Zach took his crutches to school, asked his best friend out, and started a band.

A filmmaker made a short documentary about this happy-go-lucky teenager on death row, called *My Last Days*. It showed Zach living happily, hanging out with his family, and playing music.

Everybody loved Zach. When you see the footage, you can't help but like him. As you watch him laugh and love and sing, you catch yourself forgetting: this kid is about to die.

Zach's family tells the camera how knowing he would die has helped them realize what matters in life and to find true meaning. "It's really simple, actually," Zach says. "Just try and make people happy."

As the 22-minute film closes, Zach looks into the camera, smiling, and says, "I want to be remembered as the kid who went down fighting, and didn't really lose."

Not long after he said those words, Zach passed away.

When Eli Pariser and Peter Koechley of *Upworthy* saw the film, they thought, *This is a story that needs to be heard.*

Now just over a year old, *Upworthy* has become quite popular. In fact, it recently hit 30 million monthly visitors, making it, according to the *Business Insider*, the fastest-growing media company in history.* (Seven-year-old *BuzzFeed* was serving 50 million monthly visitors at the time.)

---

* *Upworthy* has spawned dozens of imitators who have since applied its techniques to rather sneaky and cynical content. Such exploitation certainly seems more like a shortcut than a long-term smartcut, an unfortunate side effect of *Upworthy*'s success.

The Zach Sobiech story illustrates how Upworthy used rapid feedback to do it:

According to *Upworthy*'s calculations, *My Last Days* had the potential to reach a lot of people. But so far, few had seen it.

The filmmaker had posted the documentary under the headline, "*My Last Days*: Meet Zach Sobiech." Though descriptive, it was suboptimal packaging. In the ADD world of Facebook and Twitter, it's no surprise that few people clicked.

Upworthy reposted the video with a new title: "We Lost This Kid 80 Years Too Early. I'm Glad He Went Out with a Bang," and shared it with a small number of its subscribers, then waited to see who clicked.

Meanwhile, *Upworthy* sent the same video with a handful of other headlines to *different* subscribers. For example, "I Cried Through This Entire Video. That's OK Though, Because This Kid's Life Was Wonderful" and "The Happiest Story about a Kid Dying of Cancer I've Ever Seen."

Upworthy watched the "feedback" pour in, monitoring both the percentage of people who clicked each headline and the number who shared it with their friends. It was a perfect, dispassionate science experiment, where the feedback could show *Upworthy* editors exactly which packaging would have the biggest impact—before they released it to the rest of the world.

In moments, the results became clear: people clicked on the third headline 20 percent more often than the original.

But that wasn't the end of the test.

Upworthy wrote alternate versions of the winning headline and sent it out to several other groups. It repeated the process a ruthless 18 times, for a total of 75 variations in all. Here are a few of the contenders:

Headline	% Lift
We Lost This Kid 80 Years Too Early. I'm Glad He Went Out with a Bang	0%
I Cried Through This Entire Video. That's OK Though, Because This Kid's Life Was Wonderful	+9%
The Happiest Story about a Kid Dying of Cancer I've Ever Seen	+28%
RIP Amazing Rock Star Teenager Who Punched Cancer in the Face with Love on the Way Out	+65%
Cancer Wasn't a Death Sentence for This Kid. It Was a Wake Up Call.	-22%
Her Parents Asked, "Would You Date Him If He Didn't Have Cancer?" So There Ya Go.	+75%
This Kid Just Died. What He Left Behind Is Wonderful.	+96%

In the end, *Upworthy* tweaked the winning headline one more time:

Headline	% Lift
This Kid Just Died. What He Left Behind Is Wondtacular.	+116%

The winning thumbnail image—a photo of Zach and his girlfriend, foreheads touching—added another 69 percent click-through rate.

Finally, *Upworthy*'s editors were satisfied, and launched the story to the rest of their fans and the broader Internet.

This rapid feedback process didn't just increase views to the video by the calculated 186 percent, they increased views by that percentage for every *cycle* of sharers. So when you shared the video with your friends, they were three times as likely to click and share it with their friends. And those people were three times as likely to click and share. And so on.

Like The Second City, *Upworthy* turned its work into rapid, scientific experiments. It turned tiny failures into depersonalized feedback and created an environment where total failure was nearly impossible.

And in the end, more than 10 million people got to see Zach's story.

(Take that, baby meerkats!)

PART II

LEVERAGE

Sometimes the questions are complicated and the answers are simple.

—Dr. Seuss

Chapter 4

PLATFORMS

"The Laziest Programmer"

I.

The team was in third place by the time David Heinemeier Hansson leapt into the cockpit of the black-and-pink Le Mans Prototype 2 and accelerated to 120 miles per hour. A dozen drivers jostled for position at his tail. The lead car was pulling away from the pack—a full lap ahead.

This was the 6 Hours of Silverstone, a timed race held each year in Northamptonshire, UK, part of the World Endurance Championship. Heinemeier Hansson's team, Oak Racing, hoped to place well enough here to be competitive in the standings for the upcoming 24 Hours of Le Mans, the Tour de France of automobile racing.

Heinemeier Hansson was the least experienced driver among his teammates, but the Oak team had placed a third of this important race in his hands.

Determined to close the gap left by his teammate, Heinemeier Hansson put pedal to floor, hugging the curves of the 3.7-mile track that would be his singular focus for the next two hours. But as three g's of acceleration slammed into his body, he began to slide around the open cockpit. Left, then right, then left. Something was wrong with his seat.

In endurance racing, a first place car can win a six- or 12-hour race by five seconds or less. Winning comes down to two factors: the equipment and the driver. However, rules are established to ensure that every car is relatively matched, which means outcomes are determined almost entirely by the drivers' ability to focus and optimize thousands of tiny decisions.

Shifting attention from the road to, say, a maladjusted driver's seat for even a second could give another car the opportunity to pass. But at 120 miles per hour, a wrong move might mean worse than losing the trophy. As Heinemeier Hansson put it, "Either you think about the task at hand or you die."

Turn by turn, he fought centrifugal force, attempting to keep from flying out while creeping up on the ADR-Delta car in front of him.

And then it started to rain.

WHEN HEINEMEIER HANSSON WALKED onto the racing scene in his early 30s, he was a virtual unknown, both older and less experienced than almost anyone in the leagues. A native of Denmark, he's tall, with a defined jaw and dark spiky hair. At the time he raced 6 Hours of Silverstone, it had been about five years since he first drove any car at all.

That makes him one of the fastest risers in championship racing.

Despite that, Heinemeier Hansson is far better known among computer programmers—where he goes by the moniker DHH—than car enthusiasts. Though most of his fellow racers don't know it, he's indirectly responsible for the development of Twitter. And Hulu and Airbnb. And a host of other transformative technologies for which he receives no royalties. His work has contributed to revolutions, and lowered the barrier for thousands of tech companies* to launch products.

All because David Heinemeier Hansson hates to do work he doesn't have to do.

DHH lives and works by a philosophy that helps him do dramatically more with his time and effort. It's a principle that's fueled his underdog climbs in both racing and programming, and just might deliver a win for him as the cars slide around the rain-slicked Silverstone course.

But to understand his smartcut, we must first learn a little bit about how computers work.

THINK OF THE WAY a stretch of grass becomes a road. At first, the stretch is bumpy and difficult to drive over. A crew comes along and flattens the surface, making it easier to navigate. Then, someone pours gravel. Then tar. Then a layer of asphalt. A steamroller smooths it; someone paints lines. The final surface is something an automobile can traverse quickly. Gravel stabilizes, tar solidifies, asphalt reinforces, and now we don't need to build our cars to drive over bumpy grass. And we can get from Philadelphia to Chicago in a single day.

That's what computer programming is like. Like a highway, computers are layers on layers of code that make them increasingly easy to use. Computer scientists call this abstraction.

A microchip—the brain of a computer, if you will—is made of millions of little transistors, each of whose job is to turn on or off, either letting electricity flow or not. Like tiny light switches, a bunch of transistors in a computer might combine to say, "add these two numbers," or "make this part of the screen glow."

* Mine included.

In the early days, scientists built giant boards of transistors, and manually switched them on and off as they experimented with making computers do interesting things. It was hard work (and one of the reasons early computers were *enormous).*

Eventually, scientists got sick of flipping switches and poured a layer of virtual gravel that let them control the transistors by punching in 1s and 0s. 1 meant "on" and 0 meant "off." This *abstracted* the scientists from the physical switches. They called the 1s and 0s machine language.

Still, the work was agonizing. It took lots of 1s and 0s to do just about anything. And strings of numbers are really hard to stare at for hours. So, scientists created another abstraction layer, one that could translate more scrutable instructions into a lot of 1s and 0s.

This was called assembly language and it made it possible that a machine language instruction that looks like this:

10110000 01100001

could be written more like this:

MOV AL, 61h

which looks a little less robotic. Scientists could write this code more easily.

Though if you're like me, it still doesn't look fun. Soon, scientists engineered more layers, including a popular language called C, on top of assembly language, so they could type in instructions like this:

printf("Hello World");

C translates that into assembly language, which translates into 1s and 0s, which translates into little transistors popping open and closed, which eventually turn on little dots on a computer screen to display the words, "Hello World."

With abstraction, scientists built layers of road which made computer travel faster. It made the act of *using* computers faster. And new generations of computer programmers didn't need to be actual scientists. They could use high-level language to make computers do interesting things.*

When you fire up a computer, open up a Web browser, and buy a copy of this book online for a friend (please do!), you're working within a program, a layer that translates your actions into code that another layer, called an operating system (like Windows or Linux or MacOS), can interpret. That operating system is probably built on something like C, which translates to Assembly, which translates to machine language, which flips on and off a gaggle of transistors.

(Phew.)

So, why am I telling you this?

In the same way that driving on pavement makes a road trip faster, and layers of code let you work on a computer faster, hackers like DHH find and build layers of abstraction in business and life that allow them to multiply their effort.

I call these layers platforms.

AT COLLEGE IN THE early aughts, DHH was bored. Not that he couldn't handle school intellectually. He just didn't find very much of it useful.

He practiced the art of selective slacking. "Some of my proudest grades were my lowest grades," he tells me.

---

* Programmers will tell you that some computer processing speed is sacrificed when you program at higher levels. But since writing code in C is a thousand times faster than binary, it pays off.

We all know people in school and work with a masterful ability to maintain the status quo (John Bender on *The Breakfast Club* or the bald, coffee-swilling coworker from *Dilbert*), but there's a difference between treading water and methodically searching for the least wasteful way to learn something or *level up*, which is what DHH did.

"My whole thing was, if I can put in 5 percent of the effort of some-body getting an A, and I can get a C minus, that's amazing," he ex-plains. "It's certainly good enough, right? [Then] I can take the other 95 percent of the time and invest it in something I really care about."

DHH used this concept to breeze through the classes that bored him, so he could double his effort on things that mattered to him, like learning to build websites. With the time saved, he wrote code on the side.

One day, a small American Web design agency called 37signals asked DHH to build a project management tool to help organize its work. Hoping to save some time on this new project, he decided to try a relatively new programming language called Ruby, developed by a guy in Japan who liked simplicity. DHH started coding in earnest.

Despite several layers of abstraction, Ruby (and all other code lan-guages) forces programmers to make countless unimportant decisions. What do you name your databases? How do you want to configure your server? Those little things added up. And many programs re-quired repetitive coding of the same basic components every time.

That didn't jibe with DHH's selective slacking habit. "I hate repeating myself." (He almost spits on me when he says it.)

But conventional coders considered such repetition a rite of passage, a barrier to entry for newbies who hadn't paid their dues in programming. "A lot of programmers took pride in the Prot-estant work ethic, like it has to be hard otherwise it's not right," DHH says.

He thought that was stupid. "I could do a lot of other interesting things with my life," he decided. "So if programming has to be it, it has to be awesome."

So DHH built a layer on top of Ruby to automate all the repetitive tasks and arbitrary decisions he didn't want taking up his time. (It didn't *really* matter what he named his databases.) His new layer on top of programming's pavement became a set of railroad tracks that made creating a Ruby application faster. He called it Ruby on Rails.

Rails helped DHH build his project—which 37signals named Basecamp—faster than he could have otherwise. But he wasn't prepared for what happened next.

When he shared Ruby on Rails on the Internet, programmers fell in love with it. Rails was easier than regular programming, but just as powerful, so amateurs downloaded it by the thousands. Veteran coders murmured about "real programming," but many made the switch because Rails allowed them to build their projects faster.

The mentality behind Rails caught on. People started building add-ons, so that others wouldn't have to reinvent the process of coding common things like website sign-up forms or search tools. They called these "gems" and shared them around. Each contribution saved the next programmer work.

Suddenly, people were using Ruby on Rails to solve all sorts of problems they hadn't previously tackled with programming. A toilet company in Minnesota revamped its accounting system with it. A couple in New Jersey built a social network for yarn enthusiasts. Rails was so friendly that more people *became* programmers.

In 2006 a couple of guys at a podcasting startup had an idea for a side project. With Rails, they were able to build it in a few days—as an experiment—while running their business. They launched it to see what would happen. By spring 2007 the app had gotten popular enough that the team sold off the old company to pursue the side project full time. It was called Twitter.

A traditional software company might have built Twitter on a lower layer like C and taken months or years to polish it before even knowing if people would use it. Twitter—and many other successful companies—used the Rails platform to launch and validate a business idea in days. Rails translated what Twitter's programmers wanted to tell all those computer transistors to do—with relatively little effort. And that allowed them to build a company *fast*. In the world of high tech—like in racing—a tiny time advantage can mean the difference between winning and getting passed.

ISAAC NEWTON ATTRIBUTED HIS success as a scientist to "standing on the shoulders of giants"—building off of the work of great thinkers before him.

Platforms are tools and environments that let us do just that. It's clear how using platforms applies in computer programming, but what if we wanted to apply platform thinking to something outside of tech startups? Say—education?

II.

In spring 2010, Dr. Tony Wagner, a Harvard researcher, took a trip to Scandinavia to observe what was going on at schools in Finland, a country roughly the size and population of the US state of Minnesota. Finland's students consistently ranked at the top— or very near the top—each year on international mathematics, science, and reading tests. Finland had left the States—and pretty much everyone else—in the dust.

The number one ranking itself wasn't the phenomenon (somebody's got to be number one). It was that Finland somehow managed to be the best with less effort than everyone else.

Finnish students entered school one year later than most others. They took fewer classes and spent less time in school per day. They had fewer tests and less homework. And they thought school was *fun*.

Furthermore, teachers in Finland spent about half as much time each school year in the classroom, 600 hours to American teachers' 1,100.

The results of Finland's success were evident not just in students' test scores; they rippled throughout its economy. There were more researchers per capita in Finland than in any other country, and Finland ranked number one in the world in technology innovation, according to various studies. Unemployment was below average, and 82 percent of adults had the equivalent of a high school degree, which was 12 percent more than the developed world's average.

And yet, a few decades ago, Finland's education system had been decidedly mediocre. Students performed well in reading, but were average or below in just about everything else.

In other words, in a generation, Finnish education went from unremarkable to the envy of the planet. The question on Wagner's mind as his plane descended into Helsinki was, how?

"I THINK IT'S A great mistake to force children to learn mathematics," said renowned physicist Freeman Dyson, as I sat at lunch with him at the Institute for Advanced Study in Princeton, New Jersey.

Then 89, Dyson had spent the better part of a century advancing quantum electrodynamics and solid-state physics, before turning his attention to the study of game theory.

"OK," I said. "How much high-level mathematics ought to be taught in schools?"

He looked at me in between bites of swordfish. "I would put it at zero."

That's a peculiar thing for a math genius to say.

Dyson explained that it's not that we don't *need* education. "Obviously there are things that a citizen ought to know," he continued. But, "[we're using] the entirely wrong approach."

Dyson believes that American schools teach kids to, metaphorically, drive on bumpy grass instead of to pilot cars on highways. Memorization of facts and figures is the primary culprit. What we really need, he says, is to teach kids to use tools that do math for us.

In other words, no more multiplication tables. Calculators at age six. Parents and teachers, prepare your pitchforks.

Whether or not children should be allowed to use calculators in school has been a subject of hot debate since the devices became affordable. People get *upset* about it. The primary argument against calculators is a reasonable one: kids need to learn the underlying math, not just push buttons.

This debate is actually a repeat of the one that occurred in the 15th century when Italian abacists began teaching mathematics using pen and paper and formulas, instead of the traditional counting boards or piles of small objects used to calculate addition and subtraction. Scholars freaked out. They thought that formulas and algorithms would diminish one's ability to think. Of course, those things made math more powerful and gave mathematicians the ability to develop new layers of theory on top of them.

But calculators don't just help you with math. They *do* your math.

Can we really expect our kids to compete in the world marketplace by teaching them less of the hard stuff? Would one of the world's greatest mathematicians really advocate *that*?

A FEW HOURS FROM the airport from which Wagner's plane departed for Helsinki, lives a programmer named Samantha John, who had quit her job to build a computer game. From the day she had entered engineering school, she noticed how much of a minority she was: the computer science department at her college was almost exclusively male.

Many of these young men, she learned, had gotten into programming because they played video games between ages 10 and 14, and had decided they wanted to learn how to make them. If you really love video games, John pointed out, you are often curious about how to program them. "Most people don't necessarily love video games enough to want to get over that hump," she said.

She also saw that video games were often violent, involving guns and race cars and sword-wielding women in metal bikinis— not interests exclusive to boys but more likely to appeal to them. John mused, "Wouldn't it be cool if there were an engineering toy to get girls into programming?"

So she built an iPad app called Daisy the Dinosaur, where kids could begin to harness programming's concepts without having to learn its underpinnings through a series of increasingly difficult puzzles—like *Angry Birds* and the other touchscreen games kids were used to. Then she created a programming language called Hopscotch for the iPad. It allows kids to generate their own games, apps, and animations using those same puzzle-solving techniques.

In the Hopscotch language, with a couple of finger swipes, you can create an "If > Then" statement, a staple of programming logic. This might look like a cartoon squid, with a box underneath it that lets you drag commands like "Turn Right." With another swipe, you can make the squid repeat everything you dragged into the box, creating a loop, making the squid turn in circles.

This is what that MIT mathematician Seymour Papert calls constructionism, or learning by making and manipulating objects. It's incredibly effective for concept mastery and recall, and it's almost always aided by platforms.

With Hopscotch, kids have re-created their favorite video

games, built animated cartoons, and created programs that solve real-world problems. An eighth-grade class made math quizzes for their first-grade mentees, for example. One user made a spin-the-bottle app.

Many of these kids don't even know long division. But John says that's OK. "You need to know what you don't know, and how to figure it out," she explained. Hopscotch is a platform that leads kids by the hand to learn basic concepts, then encourages them to want to figure the rest out.

Instead of forcing kids to learn code through lectures and drills and mandatory classes, she built a toy that kids actually download and play with because they want to. And Hopscotch isn't the only company that's onto this idea; encouragingly, thousands of young children have learned to program video games and robots through similar constructionist games like *Gamestar Mechanic* and LEGO *Mindstorms*. A subset of those kids, Samantha says, will become passionate enough to pursue a deeper expertise in programming.

Studies show that students who use calculators have better attitudes toward math, and are more likely to pursue highly computational careers in science, technology, engineering, and mathematics (STEM) than those who don't or can't. This is certainly the case with games like John's, too.

Dyson says, and Papert confirms, that to get kids to become interested in an academic subject on their own, they have to play. Building with LEGOs, visiting museums, experimenting with tools.

Says Dyson, "Mathematics ought to be entertainment."

NOT SO FAST. IT'S great that iPads and calculators decrease effort and make some people want to learn more, but don't we need to know what we're adding and subtracting in the first place? If we use a calculator without learning math first, or a programming game without learning how code works, how are we to know when we've made a mistake?

"Part of learning the discipline is learning to communicate in the language of the discipline," says Dr. David Moursund, an emeritus professor at the University of Oregon who has authored or coauthored more than sixty books on the field of computers in education. "We want students to recognize when they encounter a math-related problem that might well be easily solvable using tools including calculators and computers."

Moursund says that before high school, we devote roughly three-quarters of our math education to memorizing and practicing the use of rules. This leaves too little time, he believes, for higher-order thinking: applying math to solving problems, creating models, or enhancing our understanding of the world. "Calculators and computers can replace some of the memorizing," he says.

"Mathematics is a way of thinking about problems and issues in the world," says Keith Devlin, Stanford executive and World Economic Forum *and* American Mathematical Society fellow.

But this, Devlin adds, is the clincher: "Get the thinking right and *the skills come largely for free.*"

The overwhelming majority of academic research about calculators indicates that leveraging such tools improves conceptual understanding. By learning the tool (calculator) first, we actually master the discipline (math) faster.

This is the point that Dyson was making earlier. Hands-on learning and the use of tools, he says, helps us to *want* to learn, to get rapid feedback, and to actually grasp math better than memorizing facts from the bottom up.

And while we may need deep expertise in our industries to become innovators, we actually need only higher-order thinking *and the ability to use platforms* to do everything else. In a pre–technology era, people with abstract knowledge were highly valued. But in the age of smartphones and Wikipedia, does it matter that you don't know offhand the name of the second-largest city in Botswana? What's important today is knowing how to use platforms to retrieve the information we need, whether it's the capital of Botswana or the result of 124,502 divided by 8.*

In an age of platforms, creative problem solving is more valuable than computational skill.

To be good citizens, responsible workers and providers, and ethical businesspeople, we need a minimum level of knowledge about the way the world works, who's in it, and how things fit together. We need to know enough about statistics to call BS on propaganda. We ought to be able to identify a good deal on a dinner menu. But what all this research tells us is that platforms can help us master those basics faster than learning the basics from scratch.

In fact, after studying decades of calculator usage in classrooms, researchers warn, "If schools do not teach students to use these devices from an early age, the rising generation will lack necessary work skills."

What this research tells us is that as the world evolves, so too should we constantly rethink our educational conventions in light of the new platforms we have. For example, today's children should be taught to use Excel spreadsheets—and all their calculations— instead of times tables. Rather than teaching a mile wide in every subject, we ought to first teach kids to use platforms, then let them go deep in the areas that interest them.

In a typical US high school, many of the teachers fall into the category of broad but shallow experts themselves. The health teacher becomes the Spanish teacher, then temporarily the geography

---

* Dudley Underwood of DePauw University put it well: "If 70% of engineers don't need calculus to do their jobs, then how many of the 500,000 students that we put through every year will?"

teacher. But, really, he's the football coach. Bless his heart, but he's basically building a road out of mud.

And that's where Finland's education system found its platform advantage.

III.

Albert Einstein is famously quoted: "The definition of insanity is doing the same thing over and over and expecting different results."

He didn't actually say it.* But in the 1990s, Finnish educators decided to take the cliché to heart.

Upon landing in Helsinki, Wagner and his crew made a beeline for some local high schools. Wagner sat among students in various classes, whispering observations to the camera like an academic version of *The Crocodile Hunter.* (When you watch the footage, you expect him to blurt out, "Krikey, look at the size of these classes!")

He explored classrooms that looked like any in America. Brick buildings. Projector screens. Preppies. Goths. Those impossible little desks.

The secret of the Finland phenomenon, Wagner discovered, was a platform it built by elevating the education level of its teachers. Finland's public school system was experiencing the same thing that made Harvard University's curriculum and network the envy of the academic world: it hired only teachers with incredible qualifications and it had them mentor students closely. Thus, students who went to school at Harvard—or in Finland—started out a rung above their peers.

---

* The original version of this oft-misattributed quote appears to be from a 1981 Narcotics Anonymous handbook.

Of course, there are incredible, qualified teachers sprinkled around the globe who do a wonderful job. But to truly raise an education system, every educator must be extremely educated. Students can't have one star teacher and a dozen mediocre instructors if they are to advance more quickly than average, as Finland's students did.

Finland made teaching jobs more desirable and job competition increased. Its standards for teachers became higher than other countries. "The whole teaching profession has been re-invented there," Wagner said. "They have much much better working conditions to prepare lessons, to collaborate with colleagues, to meet with parents and students."

Teaching in Finland became a prestigious profession where master's degrees were required to teach on every level. And only 10 percent of applicants are even chosen to begin teacher training. Once they had jobs, teachers often stayed in the profession until they retired. (Roughly half of American teachers leave in the first five years.)

Perhaps the most important benefit of having supereducated instructors is that a better-trained teacher is more adept at teaching children how to learn, whereas the coach-turned-geography-teacher will often teach *how to memorize*. Finnish education reflects that: it focuses on teaching students *how to think*, not what to think. That, says Wagner, is core to making school both interesting and valuable. As the saying, attributed to Dr. Seuss, goes: "It is better to know how to learn than to know."*

Finnish schools cut curricular fat, so they could dedicate time to training students vocational skills. Instead of abstract theory, students got hands-on practice. Instead of a surface-level understanding of every topic ever, they went deep in fewer.

---

* Everyone says it was Seuss, but the original reference is elusive.

And as you may have guessed, Finnish schools allowed students unrestricted use of calculators.

"Kids there have much more sense that they're going to have to construct their own future," Wagner says. They're taught to be entrepreneurs of their own lives. Instead of standing passively on an education assembly line and being handed reams of facts and figures, they are thrown into rooms of bricks and asked to build castles.

By teaching tools and problem solving instead of memorization and by hiring only teachers with master's degrees, Finland created a higher educational platform that gave its kids an advantage. That's how its school system shot to number one.*

For so long, "innovation" in education has amounted to more class time, more memorization, more tests. Smaller classes, but the same classes. Finland actually got better, through lateral thinking.

Edward de Bono, who coined the term "lateral thinking" in 1967, put the "Einstein" quote a bit differently: "You cannot dig a hole in a different place by digging the same hole deeper."

IV.

David Heinemeier Hansson was in a deep hole. Halfway through his stint, the sprinkling rain had become a downpour. Curve after curve, he fishtailed at high speed, still in third place, pack of hungry competitors at his rear bumper.

LMP cars run on slick tires—with no tread—for speed. The maximum surface area of the tire is gripping the road at any

---

* It should be noted that Finland's international rankings dropped a few slots in 2013. Pasi Sahlberg, author of *Finnish Lessons: What Can the World Learn about Educational Change in Finland*, attributes the slip to complacency from being at the top for so long, and the rise of other countries copying and improving on Finland's platform.

moment. But there's a reason street vehicles have grooves in them. Water on the road will send a slick tire drifting, as the smooth rubber can't channel it away. Grooved tires push water between the tread, giving some rubber grip and preventing hydroplaning. The slicker the tires—and the faster the speed—the more likely a little water will cause a car to drift.

That's exactly what was happening to the LMP racers. As the rain worsened, DHH found himself sliding around the inside of a car that was sliding all over the racetrack. Nearby, one driver lost grip, slamming into the wall.

Cars darted for the pits at the side of the track, so their teams could tear off the slick tires and attach rain tires. Rain tires are safer, but slower. And they take a precious 13-plus seconds to install. By the time the car has driven into the pits, stopped, replaced the tires, and started moving again, more than a minute can be lost.

DHH screamed into his radio to his engineer, *Should I pit in for new tires?*

LIKE I SAID, DHH wasn't the most experienced racer. He had gotten into this race because he was skilled at hacking the ladder. A few years into 37signals's success, and with Rails taking a life of its own, Hansson had started racing GT4—essentially souped-up street cars—in his spare time.

Initially, he finished in the middle of the pack with the other novices. But after studying videos of master drivers, he started placing higher. High enough that after six races, he was allowed to enter into GT3 races (the next level up), despite zero first-place wins. In GT3, he raced another six times, placing first once, third another time. He immediately parlayed up to GTE (the "E" is for "endurance"). While other racers duked it out the traditional way, spending a year in each league, and only advancing after becoming league champion, DHH "would spend exactly the shortest amount of time in any given series that I could before it was good enough to move up to the next thing."

There's no rule that says you *have* to win the championship to advance from GT4 to GT3. Nor is there a rule saying you have to spend a year in a given league before moving up. That's just the way people did it. Instead, DHH compressed what normally takes five to seven years of hard work into 18 months of smart work. "Once you stop thinking you have to follow the path that's laid out," he says, "you can really turn up the speed."

On the rainy Silverstone course, however, parlays couldn't help him anymore, and slacking was not an option. DHH had to drive as fast as safely possible, and every microsecond counted. In such tight competition, the only edge a racer had was raw driving skill.

Or, as it turned out, a better platform.

SHOULD I PIT IN? The man who hates repeating himself repeated over the radio. *I'm going to end up in the wall!*

His engineer told him to tough it out. *The rain is about to clear up.*

G-force pounding his body, DHH cautiously hugged the curves for another lap, and sure enough, the downpour began to subside. By two laps the course was dry. Heinemeier Hansson's slick tires gripped the track with more friction than his competitors' newly fitted rain tires and he sped ahead. The other drivers now had to pit *back in* for slick tires, for a total of nearly two minutes' delay that DHH entirely avoided.

At the end of his leg of the relay, DHH jumped from the car, having demolished the competition.

The slick tires provided DHH a platform advantage, more leverage to drive faster with the same pedal-to-floor effort. And though driving slick in the rain had been risky, his skill learned by imitating master racers kept him alive.

Reflecting on his rapid ascent in racing, DHH says, "You can accelerate your training if you know how to train properly, but you still don't need to be that special. I don't think I'm that special of a programmer or a businessperson or a race car driver. I just know how to train."

DHH had proven he had the skill to race. Videos of master drivers had helped him to learn quickly. His tire advantage had pushed him ahead of equally skilled drivers, and propelled him to the next level. And like Finland's higher-level educational environment, the advanced racing leagues themselves became platforms that forced him to master the basics—and faster—than he would have at a lower level.

When DHH returned to visit his home racetrack in Chicago, the same set of drivers still dominated the lower leagues.

He came back and effortlessly beat them.

AS WE'VE SEEN, PLATFORMS can take the form of tools and technology like games and tires and calculators; they can also take the form of environments like pro racing leagues or superstandard schools. In either case, the platform amplifies the effort and teaches skills in the process of using it.

Is it any wonder that nearly two-thirds of the patents filed over the last three decades came from twenty metropolitan areas with only one-third of the US population? More innovation, creativity, and art *per person* happens in large metro areas than other places; what Jonah Lehrer calls "urban friction" and Richard Florida calls the "creative class" turns cities into higher platforms for success-seekers.*

---

* There's argument as to whether a mass of creative people precedes economic growth in cities; that's a causation-versus-correlation question. But data is clear that big cities are better places for creative people to create and inventors to invent.

Platforms are why so many aspiring actors migrate to Los Angeles and why budding fashion bloggers move to New York. Platforms are why Harvard Law graduates have easier times finding jobs than those from other schools. Though it's much more difficult to get into Harvard than other law schools, you will get more leverage with a degree from Harvard. That's from a combination of Sinatra-style credibility and premium educators, both of which make up Harvard's platform.

Platforms are how Twitter could build Twitter in mere days while running a separate company. And platforms are why Finland made all its teachers get master's degrees and its students learn with hands-on tools that made learning *better.*

Effort for the sake of effort is as foolish a tradition as paying dues. How much better is hard work when it's amplified by a lever? Platforms teach us skills and allow us to focus on being great, rather than reinventing wheels or repeating ourselves.

"You can build on top of a lot of things that exist in this world," David Heinemeier Hansson told me. "Somebody goes in and does that hard, ground level science based work.

"And then on top of that," he smiles, "you build the art."

Chapter 5

WAVES

"Moore and Moore"

I.

It was summer when 16-year-old Sonny Moore finally ran away from home.

At five foot four, with pale skin, black hair, and acne, he was by no means his school football team captain. His escape from bullies who picked on him at the art academy in East Los Angeles where he studied—before his parents pulled him out for homeschooling—was music. Metal. Punk rock. Anything that rhymed with "the world doesn't understand," including a relatively new genre called screamo, which involved the scream-singing of often-depressing lyrics about death and heartache. He played along with his guitar at home and made friends with other tortured teenagers at his favorite hideout, the Internet.

Want to pull the rug out from under a tortured teen? Try telling him he's adopted. That's what Sonny's parents eventually confessed, to his horror. Identity shaken, he fought bitterly with them until getting out of L.A. seemed to be his only option for peace. He called it his "obsession."

So, when he met a sympathetic group of punk rockers from Georgia on Myspace.com—at the time, a new social network for musicians—Sonny saw an escape hatch. Full of angst, he gave Los Angeles the finger and flew, presumptuously, across the country to join the band.

Travis Richter and Matt Good were in a recording studio in Valdosta, Georgia, sorting out their first full-length rock album, when Sonny arrived. The pair, six and four years older than Sonny, respectively, had been playing music together since Sonny was a preteen, and had just signed a deal with Epitaph Records for their emo band, From First to Last. Having recorded an album's worth of music sans vocals, the rockers now had to decide which of them should be lead singer.

Full of hope for a new future as a rock guitarist, young Sonny showed up to demonstrate his skills to them. But it was too late. "Sorry, we just don't want to add another guitar to the mix," Richter told him. But Sonny had come a long way and smelled of desperation, so they let him hang around. "He was cool with it and understood, but just wanted to hang out with us anyway," Richter says.

Sonny found a place to stay and showed up to the studio day after day, eyes wide, helping out however he could.

And then one day everything changed.

"He was singing in the studio, and we were pretty surprised by his range and tone," Richter recalls. "So we had him step into the booth. As soon as he sang into the mic, we knew that he needed to be the singer." Popular emerging bands like The Used were "killing it by singing epic high notes," he explains, and Sonny's voice "fit perfectly into the new, 'screamo' style that was becoming more and more popular."

Quick etymology lesson: Screamo is like emo, but with screaming. Emo is like punk rock, but with emotional lyrics. Punk rock is like rock 'n' roll, only with faster guitars and drums and mohawks.

Early 2000s screamo was not a mainstream genre. But a certain subculture of (mostly teenage) fans obsessed over it. Sonny's voice, with Richter's and Good's guitars, nailed the sound. Everyone was excited. Especially Sonny.

From First to Last recorded his vocals, released the album, and booked a monthlong tour.

Like screamo, the Internet was experiencing its own surge among teenagers: social networking, which had brought FFTL together in the first place. As more households acquired high-speed Web access, and as playing with computers shifted from nerdy to mainstream, kids were spending more and more time in chat rooms, forums, and social networks. What started as the domain of introverts soon became *the* cool place for kids of all cliques to hang out. Whereas in the past an indie band like From First to Last could reach audiences only through expensive marketing, now it could spend all day talking to fans online.

"The idea was to mimic what was already happening on a mainstream level with pop music and boy bands as far as marketing goes," Richter explains, "and take it to the underground, which was slowly gathering and amassing on the Internet."

From First to Last invested in eyeliner, hair straighteners, piercings, and photography. "We wanted each member of the band to be a standout character and play more than just a musician's role," Richter says.

Now looking like proper rock stars, FFTL used social networks to book shows. Their self-booked tour eventually turned into a slot at the Vans Warped Tour. At every show, the band promoted its social networking pages, and its popularity surged as fans shared the music with their friends. "The whole emo/post-hardcore trend exploded because of the Internet," Richter says. "You go to school all day and still deal with the food-chain mentality, but with the Internet you could be whoever you wanted and anti-mainstream."

This was a disruptive moment for the music industry. Independent bands could suddenly gain a wide audience on an extremely lean budget, and new genres could find fans before a record label invested in an edgy new band.

FFTL was one of the first bands to prove the model.

"We sold like, probably at this point, over half a million units between two records," Sonny tells me, recalling the band's status after its second album, *Heroine*, dropped in 2006. "[With] no major press." The ripple effect—amplified by the growth of both screamo and the Web—had made FFTL, at the time, one of the biggest indie bands out there.

They started getting phone calls from bigger record companies.

"That courting experience was wild," Richter recalls. "Every major label was hitting us up, flying us out, flying out to our shows, taking us out to dinner, taking us shopping." When the executives asked the lip-pierced screamo kids to name their price for a record contract, Richter said, "Seven million."

Capitol Records smoothly agreed to the number. Perhaps a little too smoothly.

II.

It's a rare gloomy day at Huntington Beach, California, and Carissa Moore and Coco Ho are floating five feet apart in the middle of the ocean, trying not to look at each other.

The two Hawaiians bob with the tide, scanning the gray horizon, Ho with her black wetsuit and a tall ponytail, and Moore in pink and gray. A hundred yards behind them, muted and out of focus, a mob of bystanders—tens of thousands—scream. What happens in the next 20 minutes will determine who will go back home and who will move on to the semifinals—and eventually finals—of the Vans US Open of Surfing, and possibly who will become the women's surf world champion.

Currently, Coco Ho is leading the heat, having scored an 8.0 (out of 10) by carving up the face of the most recent, decent wave. The competitors are graded by their two best scores within a 30-minute period.

Abruptly, both women turn their surfboards toward shore. A wave is coming, but as it approaches, the surge looks iffy. Ho backs off.

Moore, however, paddles furiously. As the water rises to a peak, forming a near-vertical face, she stands up. The wave becomes the blade of a bulldozer, shoving Moore forward. She glides through the froth and cuts sharply left to speed down the open face of the wave, emerging from the spray to ride directly in front of the surging peel. From the shore, it looks like the wave is crumbling from left to right, and Moore is floating on the edge of the crumble.

She twists her surfboard to carve up the wave, then pivots forward to speed down the face again, snapping her fins above the water in a brief moment of weightlessness. Two more times she carves like this before the peel overtakes her. She turns her board into the froth to paddle back out.

Ho continues to bob in the distance. The judges announce Moore's score: 9.5

The clock ticks away. Twenty minutes pass, with no change in the standings. Moore has returned to her original waiting spot. As the timer nears zero, another wave materializes. In a flash, she grabs it in the brief window before Ho spots the opportunity. The water whisks Moore away once more, while Ho paddles around, looking for a wave that can help her beat a 9.5.

That wave finally comes at the buzzer. Frustratingly, Ho sees it late. She swims for it, but she's too far out in the water. It passes. The round is over.

The two women—who are friends when not competing against each other—swim to shore together. Both are top contenders in the surfing world tour and have faced off dozens of times in high-pressure competitions like this. Both are in their early twenties, and either could outsurf any human on the planet—with the exception of a few of the top-ranked male surfers.

But as one of the event announcers, Leila Hurst, points out, world championships aren't won by surfing skill, and this heat was no exception.

"It's really not about surfing and practicing," Hurst says, on air. "It's just a matter of waiting for the right wave."

THE DIFFERENCE BETWEEN CATCHING a wave and getting crushed or passed by is a matter of centimeters, which means the chance of being in the exact right spot in that water to grab a big wave without *any* effort is akin to winning at Powerball. Being in the water when a good wave comes requires maneuvering into precise position.

Surfers make it look easy. The good ones can recognize the roll of incoming waves, so they can position themselves in the perfect spot to catch them. And at the last minute, a surfer will paddle vigorously to align herself with the wave and match its speed.

Luck is often talked about as "being in the right place at the right time." But like a surfer, some people—and companies—are adept at *placing themselves at the right place at the right time.* They seek out opportunity rather than wait for it.

This chapter is about hacking that process.

QUICK SCIENCE REFRESHER: A wave is made up of alternating crests and troughs that from the side look like a squiggly line. When two waves collide, one of two things can happen: they can cancel each other out or, if timed just right, they can combine and increase in intensity.

This is called destructive and constructive interference. The former means the waves collide and go flat. The latter forms a megawave.

In 2004 two waves collided in American teen culture, resulting in a fast and powerful megawave. Those waves were social networking and screamo. From First to Last happened to be in the water when the megawave came, and had the foresight to paddle for it.

But the waves with the tallest crests also have the deepest troughs. By 2007 the wave that took FFTL so far so quickly was about to dump the bandmates off their boards. Soon after signing the band, Capitol Records, which was struggling like other labels in the new Internet economy of iTunes and Pandora, embarked on a large and messy merger.

Hundreds of Capitol staff members were cut. Artist contracts started getting dropped. The newly minted, makeup-wearing screamo kids from Georgia got caught in the turbulence.

"There was so much label fallout," Sonny said. "People getting fired. There was a lot of negativity."

The band started to panic. That $7 million chest of money seemed to be disappearing among a sea of middlemen. The glue holding the FFTL surfboard together was starting to disintegrate.

Richter and the others wanted to try to ride it out. But, rather than fall into the impending trough and get crushed by the wave, 18-year-old Sonny decided to bail.

III.

There are two ways to catch a wave: exhausting hard work—paddling—and pattern recognition—spotting a wave early and casually drifting to the sweet spot. "There are people who make careers based on the fact that they know how to read the ocean better than others," says Pat O'Connell, '90s surfing legend and trainer. "It's just about knowing the ocean. It's timing."

Sonny Moore seemed to have that pattern recognition; he spotted the rise of social networks and became a power user, ultimately setting himself up to front an emerging band. From First to Last spotted the fast rise of screamo before most bands—and mainstream audiences—saw it coming. When Sonny recognized that the end was near, he got off the wave.

The real question is, was that all just luck? Was Sonny just a natural? Or can such wavespotting be taught?

SOME TIME AGO, DRS. Erik Dane, Kevin Rockmann, and Michael Pratt, researchers in organizational behavior and human decision making, recruited a couple hundred college students to watch clips from some basketball games for extra credit in their business classes. Some of the students had played several years of basketball—the researchers called them "high expertise." The rest were relative newbies.

The researchers sat the students down and instructed them to watch video clips from two college basketball games and rate the difficulty of each shot a player took. Half the students were instructed to make their assessments using intuition—the first thought they had—and half were instructed to use careful analytical reasoning to judge each shot and to ignore "gut instincts." Before the test began, the second group created lists of factors from which to assess the shots, things like the number of nearby defenders, whether the shooter was stationary, and how many points the shot was worth. Answers would be compared to a key created by top basketball coaches.

When the results from the intuition test came back, the high-expertise students performed close to 50 percent better than those with low expertise. As one might expect.

The surprise came on the analytical test, where the high- and low-expertise students scored nearly the same, and *better than the high-expertise students' intuition.*

The low-expertise students who used their guts to guess at a shot's difficulty did poorly, as expected. But when these same students used thoughtful criteria, they outperformed the intuition of experienced players.

The researchers then conducted a similar experiment where they asked people to identify counterfeit handbags. "High-expertise" individuals were identified by how many Coach and Louis Vuitton handbags they owned. The results were the same.

In a given domain—be it surfing or accounting or political fund-raising—the familiarity that leads to pattern recognition seems to come with experience and practice. Fencing masters recognize opportunities in opponents' moves because of the sheer amount of practice time logged into their heads. Leaders and managers who use their gut to make decisions often do so based on decades of experience, archived and filed away in the folds of their cerebrums.

"Intuition is the result of nonconscious pattern recognition," Dane tells me. However, his research shows that, while logging hours of practice helps us see patterns subconsciously, we can often do just as well by deliberately looking for them. In many fields, such pattern hunting and deliberate analysis can yield results just as in the basketball example—high accuracy on the first try.

And that's where, like the dues-paying presidents or overly patient programmers, what we take for granted often gets in the way of our own success. Deliberate pattern spotting can compensate for experience. But we often don't even give it a shot.

This explains how so many inexperienced companies and entrepreneurs beat the norm and build businesses that disrupt established players. Through deliberate analysis, the little guy can spot waves better than the big company that relies on experience and instinct once it's at the top. And a wave can take an amateur farther faster than an expert can swim.

It also explains why the world's best surfers arrive at the beach hours before a competition and stare at the ocean.

After years of practice, a surfer can "feel" the ocean, and intuitively find waves. But the best surfers, the ones who win championships, are tireless students of the sea.

O'Connell says, "One of the main things that you do when you learn to compete is learn how to pick out conditions. Know that the tide is getting higher. Counting waves, how many waves come into a particular area that fit your eye that you want to ride."

Pro surfers analyze the frequency of waves coming in on a given day, where along the coast they tend to break, and which of those waves tend to look the best. They take note of the direction the waves break, the angle at which they peel, and where along the horizon the good ones first form.

On the other hand, sometimes the biggest waves form out of seemingly nowhere. A superwave can show up on a regular surf day when random smaller waves align. When that happens, the only people who can possibly ride it are the ones who actually went to the beach that day. The ones who actually got in the water.

BY THE END OF 2012 Google's Gmail service had become the most popular electronic mail provider in the world. That same year, Google's AdSense product accounted for more than $12 billion in revenue, about a quarter of the search giant's total revenues. Each of those products—smart electronic mail and context-based advertising—caught an enormous wave when it launched.

Like Twitter, as we learned in chapter 4, both Gmail and AdSense started off as side projects. Google was in the water when the waves of Internet traffic came because it was tinkering with new ideas under the umbrella of Google's famous "20% Time."

"20% Time" is not Google indigenous. It was borrowed from a company formerly known as Minnesota Mining and Manufacturing, aka 3M, which allowed its employees to spend 15 percent of their work hours experimenting with new ideas, no questions asked. 3M's "15% Time" brought us, among other things, Post-it Notes.

Behind this concept (which is meticulously outlined in an excellent book by Ryan Tate called *The 20% Doctrine*) is the idea of constantly tinkering with potential trends—having a toe in interesting waters in case waves form.

This kind of budgeted experimentation helps businesses avoid being disrupted, by helping them harness waves on which younger competitors might otherwise use to ride past them. It's helped companies like Google, 3M, Flickr, Condé Nast, and NPR remain innovative even as peer companies plateaued. In contrast, companies that are too focused on defending their current business practice and too fearful to experiment often get overtaken. For example, lack of experimentation in digital media has cost photo brand Kodak nearly $30 billion in market capitalization since the digital photography wave overwhelmed it in the late '90s.

The best way to be in the water when the wave comes is to budget time for swimming.

IV.

Over the years, entrepreneurs and academics have suggested that first movers in business—the first to catch a commercial wave—enjoy an unfair advantage over their competitors. In 1988 Stanford professors Marvin Lieberman and David Montgomery popularized the concept, suggesting that the first competitor to move into a market has the opportunity to gain proprietary learning, snatch up patents, and build up buyer switching costs. Later researchers added that first movers receive outsize branding benefits, that a reputation for being "the original," often enjoys a marketing advantage over copycats. (Think Tylenol versus generic acetaminophen. Or Apple's iPad versus other tablets that came after it.)

"The first mover advantage is huge," declared venture capitalist Ken Lerer. I wrote his quote down in enormous letters in my notebook when he emphatically said it to a group of fellow entrepreneurship-curious journalists when I was a student at Columbia University. According to Lerer, when we look at history—and emerging competitions—we ought to expect the first mover to win a disproportionate amount of the time.

Except if we did, we'd be wrong.

CARISSA MOORE IS BACK in the water again. Paddling to her right is local Southern California heroine Courtney Conlogue, a rising star who's been killing the competition this week at her home beach.

These are the US Open of Surfing finals. The woman who surfs the best in the next 30 minutes will take home a $15,000 check. A win would also place Moore back at the top of the world rankings. Last year's world champ and runner-up have both been eliminated, but Conlogue's blond hair is still wet from when she destroyed the then world number one, Tyler Wright, an hour and a half before.

An X-Games gold medalist and Orange County Female Surfer of the Year, Conlogue had beaten Moore soundly in a competition in New Zealand earlier that year.

At age 18, Moore had won the record for being the youngest women's surfing world champion in history. But the glory didn't last long: A year later, she had slipped to third place in the world tour. This heat could bring her back to the top . . . or sink her further.

Like sharks in water, the two competitors drift. A lump forms on the horizon; both paddle for position at the potential break point. As the lump becomes a roiling peak, neither woman backs down. Each jockeys for position, and the peak forms directly between them. Conlogue splits left, and Moore splits right. The wave closes out to the left, but Moore manages to get three moves in. She cuts right then left then right as the face turns to foam. She scores a 7.83 to Conlogue's disappointing 0.5. The ride gives Moore the lead.

Conlogue gets back in position and waits. The next big wave arrives—a fast lefthander—and she rides it into the pier, performing a few turns before it goes soft. The judges award her a 6.10, putting her four-and-a-half points behind Moore's total.

But what Conlogue doesn't see is an even bigger wave forming in the distance.

Moore knew it was coming. Having let the previous wave go by, she gracefully pushes her board out in front of this better wave, stands, speeds down the face, and carves back up it like a ramp. She catches air, her surfboard fins clearing the lip, and slams back down the face with authority.

The judges give her a 6.50.

The pier above is packed tightly with spectators as Conlogue paddles out from under it to intercept Moore's return swim. A wave rolls in—it looks like something I would paddle for myself—but neither woman pays it any mind. It turns out to be fat, not breaking until close to shore.

Conlogue catches three smaller waves in the frantic final minute, but her capable rides aren't sufficient to pass Moore's total score. The judges call out the final tally as Moore's coach runs out to the shallow water to greet her. The crowd picks Moore up on its shoulders and chairs her up the beach, tossing a purple flower lei around her neck.

To win the championship, Moore harnessed the phenomenon of wave trains. Unlike coloring-book waves, beach breaks are not composed of perfectly identical troughs and crests. They're inter-mittent, choppy, highly variable.

On good wave days, an ocean swell will bring in a massive amount of energy from some faraway place, a moving, macrolump in the ocean. Within that swell are essentially ripples, small waves and big waves that come in groups and often repeat in patterns. Waves on waves on waves. Surfers call these patterns "sets." A set might consist of one or two or three surfable waves in a row, followed by some period of silence or small waves, before another set rolls in. Often, multiwave sets consist of "forerunners" or fast-moving, but smaller waves, followed by slow-moving waves which contain the peak energy of the swell.

Since wave patterns play out over long periods of time and often behave unpredictably as waves from different directions meet and create interference, it's easy to miss the train for the waves. In all her heats of the US Open—and especially the finals—Moore benefited from deliberate study of the patterns, which helped her make the smartest wave selections.

"Before my heats at the Open, I watched the lineup and figured out which peaks were the most consistent with good waves," she told me. "When I was out there, I usually began judging a wave as soon as I saw a lump forming in the horizon." This study allowed her to beat the hometown hero Conlogue, who certainly had developed intuition on this beach from years of surfing there. Did Moore beat Conlogue because the former studied the waves harder that day, while the latter took her experience in these waves for granted? It appears so.

We also see from Moore's championship heat that, in surfing, the first mover often doesn't have the advantage. The second or third wave in a multiwave set is often the more powerful.

Perhaps we shouldn't be surprised to learn, then, that being the first mover is not much of an advantage in business either.

A DECADE AFTER LIEBERMAN and Montgomery convinced the business world of the phenomenon of first-mover advantage, they qualified their conclusions, saying, "Pioneers often miss the best opportunities, which are obscured by technological and market uncertainties. In effect, early entrants may acquire the 'wrong' resources, which prove to be of limited value as the market evolves."

Another academic duo, Peter Golder and Gerard Tellis of the University of Southern California, published a study in 1993 to see if historical evidence backed the claim that market pioneers were more likely to succeed. They researched what happened to 500 brands in 50 product categories, from toothpaste to video recorders to fax machines to chewing gum.

Startlingly, the research showed that 47 percent of first movers *failed*. Only about half the companies that started selling a product first remained the market leader five years later, and only 11 percent of first movers remained market leaders over the long term.

By contrast, early leaders—companies that took control of a product's market share after the first movers pioneered them—had only an 8 percent failure rate. Fifty-three percent of the time in the Golder and Tellis study, an early leader became the market leader in a category.

Like early pioneers crossing the American plains, first movers have to create their own wagon trails, but later movers can follow in the ruts. First movers take on the burden of educating customers, setting up infrastructure, getting regulatory approvals, and making mistakes—getting feedback and adjusting.

Fast followers, on the other hand, benefit from free-rider effects. The pioneers clear the way in terms of market education and infrastructure and learn the hard lessons, so the next guys can steal what works, learn objectively from the first movers' failures, and spend more effort elsewhere. The first wave clears the way for a more powerful ride.

Many of the biggest corporate successes in history—including Lerer's *Huffington Post*, which became the number one political website in the world, the first for-profit online-only newspaper to win a Pulitzer Prize for reporting, and which sold for more than $300 million to AOL—have been fast followers in their respective spaces. As entrepreneurship scholar Steve Blank points out in his article for *Business Insider*, "You're Better Off Being a Fast Follower Than an Originator," fast follower General Motors surpassed the first mover in automobiles, Ford Motor Company, in market share in the early 1900s. Google, Facebook, and Microsoft were each fast followers in their respective spaces in the technology sector, leaping past Overture, Myspace, and Apple, respectively (until Apple made a comeback).

In each case, while the pioneers were entrenched in early

technology and practices, the tailgaters got ahead. Once you jump on the first wave, it's costly to back off from the commitment. And by that time it's usually too late to take advantage of the second wave.

Of course, on rare occasions that first wave actually *is* the best wave in a set. How is a surfer, much less a businessperson, to judge when to make a move?

Pattern recognition can help here as well. The way to predict the best waves in a proverbial set is established by researchers Fernando F. Suarez and Gianvito Lanzolla, who in *Academy of Management Review* explain that when market and technology growth are smooth and steady, the first mover gets the inertia and an advantage. When industry change is choppy, the fast follower—the second mover—gets the benefits of the first mover's pioneering work and often catches a bigger wave, unencumbered.

A good surfer watches the conditions and knows if the big waves come alone, in smooth and steady progressions, or in patterned sets, in which case the second or third wave is often the biggest ride. And if he watches long enough, he can spot the double waves that occasionally combine to form a monster.

V.

After leaving From First to Last in 2007, Sonny Moore went from sleeping in luxurious hotels around the world and playing sold-out stadium shows to living in a warehouse in Los Angeles in a matter of months. FFTL's seven-figure contract had ended in a puff of smoke as the Capitol merger problems metastasized, and the label dropped the band.

Needless to say, Sonny was sour on the business of music.

He briefly tried his hand at a solo career, vowing to leave agents and labels out of the equation. But with vocal cord problems and no wave to push him further than his savings account could carry him, he was now back in L.A. with no plan, sitting on the floor of a warehouse with a laptop computer.

By that time, personal computers and cheap software were starting to match professional studios in recording and mixing quality, and digital instruments allowed the computer-savvy to create almost any sound imaginable. So, Sonny, fresh off a series of vocal cord surgeries, started recording music on his laptop. No band. No singing. No label. Just electronic instruments he could power with keyboard and mouse.

And he kind of liked it.

"I had a neighbor who DJed," Sonny remembered. "And I would go over and just jam. I didn't know DJing was even a thing." Sonny would show his neighbor his new, digital songs. "He'd be like, 'this is solid.'"

They started throwing warehouse dance parties, to share their music with friends. Soon, music-scene kids from downtown L.A. started showing up. Electronic musicians started offering to collaborate on tracks; Sonny connected online with DJs around the world who seemed to be popping out of nowhere. Before he knew it, Sonny found himself paddling straight into an electronic-music swell.

"That whole wave ended up being massive," he said.

It's a rare cool August evening on Randall's Island in New York City, a smallish swatch of land sticking out of the East River between Manhattan and Queens, and I'm standing in a pool of water in front of the speakers at one of Sonny's dance parties. Sonny and his friend Alex Ridha (known in the music community as Boys Noize) are above me on the DJ platform, peeking out over a snarl of cords, a mixer, and four electronic turntables. Behind me, lurching to the drum-and-bass that throbs out of Sonny's speakers, partygoers are indeed dancing.

Only unlike most dance parties I'd been to, the attendee count for this shindig is approximately 100,000.

I turn my back to the speakers to soak in the spectacle. A sea of humans unfolds, extending so far that I expect it to disappear over the curvature of the earth. The collective bounces in rhythm, a blur of neon green and a hue that I can only describe as "shirtless white guy." Someone in the back is waving an American flag on a banner, while someone else holds up the Union Jack. A giant brown Japanese cartoon monster bobs above the mohawked and pigtailed heads to the right, held up on a stick, and a dozen balloons bounce above the crowd, illuminated by a massive array of seizure-inducing strobe lights and LEDs. Half the audience wears 3-D glasses.

The massive wave Sonny had mentioned was a new genre of popular music called EDM—electronic dance music. The genre exploded faster in Europe and America than almost any other musical style had in recent decades. A combination of the Internet's disruption of traditional music distribution (services allowing artists to sell individual tracks without middlemen) and the rise of more viral-ready networking platforms (sites that connected artists to millions at a scale that early music networks didn't) created a musical wave that approached consumers from the north, while an appetite for electronic music—and the tools to create it—created a wave from the east. They combined to form the superwave that Sonny Moore managed to hop on at exactly the right time.

While living in that warehouse, Sonny had started releasing his EDM tracks online, for free. It was good stuff, and between the parties and social networks, his body of work started to gain recognition.

One day a producer approached him, asking if he'd like to remix a record for an up-and-coming artist named Lady Gaga.

"This was right before she really exploded," Sonny says. He recognized the cultural jetstream Gaga was busy creating with her dance-and-art-infused pop, and said, *Yes*.

Gaga became one of the first musicians to bring EDM from underground to mainstream, dominating the music charts and racking up half a billion views to her video for "Bad Romance" on YouTube, the hit single that Sonny had just remixed.

And once again, things got crazy.

I TURN TO FACE the stage, which rests on top of an array of speakers the breadth of a New York City block. The bass is so powerful that it sprays droplets of water on me with every thump. The treble slamming out of the speaker cones is the sound of a million defibrillators being jammed by alien radio transmissions. The hairs on my arms dance with the sheer vibration as I, alone in the security moat between stage and crowd, raise my camera and notepad to document the scene. Above, Sonny Moore, now the artist known as Skrillex, headbangs over his turntables, his 15-inch-long hair flying against a backdrop of white electricity.

In the past three years, Skrillex has won six Grammys, including best dance/electronica album twice in a row (and a nomination for best new artist), and has come to symbolize a genre into which thousands of artists—and millions of fans—are flooding.

"He is this generation's Kurt Cobain," says Joe Villacrusis, tour manager and music industry veteran who's traveled with and babysat rock stars since the early '90s. "Look at the history of music . . . he's the face of a movement."

The once-king of screamo was now the king of dubstep, having caught not one, but two gigantic musical waves in less than a decade. Sonny certainly wasn't the first mover in either genre, as artists had been pioneering—struggling to break ground on—emo, screamo, EDM, and dubstep for years before the styles reached an inflection point with listeners. He hopped on board for the second wave and paddled hard for it each time.

From First to Last sold a respectable 500,000 records. By now, Skrillex has sold more than 2 million. And his success has gone deeper than money and fame. Just before the Randall's Island show, Sonny landed from a humanitarian trip to Africa for the nonprofit "(RED)" and, perhaps more importantly, had found peace in his life. He'd repaired the relationship with his parents. (His dad now hangs out regularly with Sonny's music crew.) And whereas he'd spent most of his life with long hair covering up his acne scars, Sonny shaved one side of his head, unafraid to be himself and to be seen. The look soon became iconic.

A casual observer might conclude that Sonny just happened to be in the right place at the right time, two times. That he was just lucky. But that's not what happened. Sonny actively experimented with trends when they were still early—the Web, social networks, scream-singing, EDM—sticking his toe in different waters until he recognized incoming waves. And it should be noted that he tried some things that didn't work (a solo career as a rock singer) and was quick to shift strategies.

Conventional thinking leads talented and driven people to believe that if they simply work hard, luck will eventually strike. That's like saying if a surfer treads water in the same spot for long enough, a wave will come; it certainly happens to *some* people, once in a while, but it's not the most effective strategy for success. Paradoxically, it's actually a lazier move.

There's a reason some people practice things for twenty years and never become experts; a golfer can put in 30,000 hours of practice and not improve his game if he's gripping his clubs wrong the whole time. A business can work five times harder and longer than its neighbors and still lose to rivals that read the market better. Just like a pro surfer never wins by staying in one spot.

"I think that being able to pick and read good waves is almost more important than surfing well," Moore tells me. "If you don't have a good or better platform to perform on than your opponent, you are going to lose."

Her secret, and Sonny's (and Google's and 3M's and General Motors'), isn't practice—though that certainly helps. It's going to the beach to watch the waves and getting into the water to experiment.

And if you're in the sweet spot when that superwave does come, Sonny says, "It's pure energy."

Chapter 6

SUPERCONNECTORS

"Space, Wars, and Storytellers"

I.

Playa Las Coloradas, on the southern coast of the island of Cuba, is named for a density of red mangrove trees—*mangle rojo*—which thrive in marshy water and beneath olive-colored bark reveal red wood. Up the road, the sleepy town of Niquero sits peacefully with its eclectic mix of Spanish colonial buildings, Victorian houses, and plantation manors. To the east, the interior yields miles of sugarcane fields. Beyond the fields lie the Sierra Maestra mountains, a cave-ridden range with luscious jungle and majestic slopes crafted over millennia by earthquakes, volcanoes, and tsunamis. To the west, the white-sand shore stares out at an endless green-blue Caribbean.

On December 2, 1956, a leaky yacht from Mexico, christened the *Granma*, churned into view of that shore.

From it sprang 82 men, a starving band of former Cuban university students and expats. Having crammed together on that boat for seven days, they were delighted to set their wobbly sea legs on land, but perhaps dismissed the *mangle rojo* as they shouldered their backpacks and beelined into the sugar fields.

They weren't sightseeing. They were there for a revolution.

Exiled from their homeland after the military tossed Cuban democracy out to sea, this little band was hoping to surprise a military stronghold while a handful of sympathetic saboteurs created a diversion inside the populous nearby city of Santiago. This was to be the spark that would inspire the oppressed Cuban peasantry to take back their country.

Except the revolutionaries were the ones about to be surprised. Having been tipped off, soldiers awaited the seafaring rebels in the fields beyond the beach.

CUBA WAS NO STRANGER to revolution. Fifty-eight years before, the people had wrested their country from colonial Spain, which had occupied Cuba for almost all the years since Christopher Columbus discovered it and had introduced a massively profitable slave and sugar trade. In the late 19th century, led by the national hero José Martí—the George Washington of Cuba, if you will—rebellion gained the support of the United States, sparked the Spanish-American War, and led Spain to withdraw from the island. Yet even after Cuba gained independence in 1902, infighting, insurrection, and civil war plagued the Caribbean's largest island for decades.

By 1940 Cuba had made some progress. It had a constitution and free elections; however, the fledgling democracy was plagued by political and economic corruption. Then in 1952 a military man named Fulgencio Batista decided to cancel the next election.

Batista was a gangster. With heavy support from the United States—whose investors owned nearly all the power and telephone industries in the country, and who had held Cuba's trade-dependent economy by the throat since the Spaniards left—Batista's island became a haven for the American mob, which embedded casinos and brothels into the fabric of Cuban cities like

Havana and Santiago. The working and rural class—the vast majority of Cubans—suffered and starved. Though it claimed to be a democracy, the new Cuba was a military dictatorship. Batista censored the media. The police harassed and detained critics and journalists. The military executed politically active students who dared to speak negatively of the state.

Three years before he leapt off *Granma* at Playa Las Coloradas, a 26-year-old Fidel Castro had led a group of such idealistic academics in a naive confrontation at a military barracks in Moncada, a gesture he hoped would initiate an uprising and eventual restoration of the government to the Cuban people. The attack failed and Castro was imprisoned.

"Condemn me. It does not matter," Castro said at his trial in a lengthy but eloquent denunciation of the Batista regime. He admitted his hand in the attack, but argued boldly for the restoration of Cuba to its people. Declaring that the authority of government should come from the consent of the governed, he quoted the Cuban Constitution, the US Declaration of Independence, Martin Luther, and St. Thomas Aquinas. "History will absolve me," he said.

Perhaps mercifully, or perhaps exasperated and not wishing to create a martyr, Batista had released Castro in 1955 as part of an amnesty of political prisoners. Castro and many of his rebellious fellows went into exile in Mexico. Batista would, hopefully, never have to deal with their irritating populist rhetoric again.

And now those rebellious fellows had returned, though things were going badly for them.

Castro had spent the time since his release attempting to raise money and support for a Cuban revolution throughout the United States and Mexico. He was spurned by each, and routinely harassed by Batista agents in Mexico. Both the USSR and Cuba's communist party wanted nothing to do with Fidel's little revolt, which wasn't about the socialism that Cold War–era America would grow to fear, but instead about taking power out of the corrupt hands of the dictatorship and the mob. Finally, the ousted former president of Cuba, Carlos Prío Socarrás, who now lived in Florida, slipped Castro enough money to buy a boat.

The boat was *Granma*, a 13-year-old, 60-foot yacht made to accommodate, at most, about 20 people. Fidel stuffed 82 on board and cast off at 1:30 a.m. on a November night in 1956. Destination: the southeastern coast of Cuba.

Soon after the would-be revolutionaries hit the shore, the Batista army hit them. Hungry, seasick, and outnumbered, Castro's crew was wrecked; some 60 to 65 of them killed, either immediately, or after being scattered and pursued. Fidel, his brother Raul, and a dozen remaining men escaped into the jungle. As the rebels staggered through forests and up slopes and past rural villages, attempting to regroup, the Batista government reported how it had crushed the *Granma* rebellion and "killed" its leaders.

The last part, at least, wasn't true.

Castro and the remaining outlaws made camp in the Sierra Maestra, foraging for food and sneaking out of the woods at night to steal ammunition from Batista outposts. Led by the group's doctor, an idealistic Argentine named Ernesto Guevara (the Cubans called him Che) who, it turned out, had a knack for guerrilla warfare, the little band began sabotaging Batista facilities and taking small military squads by surprise—hitting targets one-by-one and fading into the jungle. The rebels made bombs out of soup cans and Molotov cocktails from rum bottles. They established a small "liberated area" that they declared sovereign territory. They gathered disenchanted peasants from the rural areas, trained them to fight, and grew ranks to 300 guerrilla soldiers.

They were a tiny, hopeless group. Three hundred was nothing compared to Batista's army occupying the island's 42,000 other square miles. And Batista had tanks and planes. At the current rate, the rebels would die of old age before they wore down the enemy. And in the meantime, millions of Cuban citizens for whom they were fighting didn't know the rebels existed. The only sign of this handful of unshaven idealists came from the occasional rat-tat-tat of gunfire in the distance, muted by a hundred miles of fog and sugarcane fields.

Then one day some of Dr. Guevara's men showed up to the rebel camp with a device that would change the revolution.

WHICH IS EASIER—MAKING FRIENDS with a thousand people one by one or making friends with someone who already has a thousand friends? Which is faster—going door to door with a message or broadcasting the message to a million homes at once?

This is the idea behind what I call superconnecting, the act of making mass connections by tapping into hubs with many spokes. It's what Castro needed to do if he ever wanted to convert the Cuban people to his cause.

Imagine you're at a party and you don't know any of the other guests. You look around at the dozens of people and, if you're extroverted, you'll probably strike up a conversation with someone nearby. If you're a little more timid in unfamiliar territory like I am, you might wander around in hopes that someone strikes up a conversation with *you*.

Now imagine that a friend of yours shows up. She happens to know everybody at the party and she decides to take you around and meet everyone whom you should know. You soon meet a dozen people, with very little effort. Your friend is a superconnector.[*]

---

[*] Superconnectors are a subset of the "Connectors" Malcolm Gladwell writes about in *The Tipping Point*, people whose many acquaintances span social circles and who can facilitate in the spreading of ideas and epidemics. While Connectors are often passive links between groups, superconnectors actively use their networks to help individuals *reach* many people at once. For a bonus discussion on Gladwell and superconnectors, check out shanesnow.com/superconnectors.

That's the role that mass media has played in our lives for the past two centuries—superconnecting sources of information to relevant audiences all at once and superconnecting businesses to millions of potential customers through advertising.

Before newspapers could reach hundreds of thousands of people in a day and before radio and television and Internet publishing could reach millions at once, there were few national- or international-scale businesses. And there certainly weren't fast-growing startups and consumer brands in the numbers we see today. But once companies could communicate to many, the number of fast-growing and large-scale businesses in the world skyrocketed.

That was the kind of influence the Castro brothers attained when Che Guevara brought the contraband equipment to their mountain camp in February 1958. The device that helped turn the tide of the revolution, if you hadn't guessed, was a radio transmitter.

WHEN THE CUBAN REBELS began broadcasting in February 1958, radio had the most reach of any medium in Latin America. Much of the population was too poor to afford television, lived too far out in the countryside to receive newspapers, or simply couldn't read. And as the rebels correctly theorized, the urban poor and rural peasantry would be crucial to overthrowing Batista's brutal regime.

The first broadcast from Guevara's ham radio transmitter only went a few hundred yards. But with a little work—Guevara recruited a technician, a newspaper reporter, and a couple of radio announcers from among rebel supporters in nearby villages—he could broadcast to nearby towns, and eventually, after secretly airlifting in more powerful equipment, the entire island. Every broadcast started the same way, "Aqui Radio Rebelde! Transmitiendo desde la Sierra Maestra en territorio libre de Cuba."

The goal was to shed light on what was really happening in Cuba, and to inspire potential supporters to spread the "Free Cuba" message. Each day, Radio Rebelde transmitted reports of Batista troop movements and the military skirmishes the rebels had with them. Castro and his lieutenants gave speeches, local musicians played patriotic songs, and soldiers delivered personal messages to their families. When revolution supporters were arrested in a given city, Radio Rebelde announced the names, hoping to galvanize local outrage. The rebels let the islanders know that someone was out there fighting for them and detailed the horrors Batista wreaked on Cuba's citizens. Batista's credibility eroded.

Radio Rebelde became a formidable weapon for the revolution, and "made concrete to the whole nation the most far-reaching and resonant events in the armed struggle against the Batista dictatorship," wrote rebel soldier Ricardo Martinez Victores. "Each night, the air of the island thrummed to the radio waves of the world of the Sierra Maestra, cascading down onto the citizens of the plains and cities."

Every night, Cubans in the cities and Cubans in the fields huddled around their radios for those words, "Aqui Radio Rebelde!" Even Batista's jailed political enemies furtively tuned in from their cells, waiting for the moment when perhaps they could distract the government from the inside.

"The fact that we were outnumbered so greatly by Batista's army did not deter us," said William Gálvez Rodriguez, a young activist who heard the Radio Rebelde and joined the movement, eventually becoming a captain of the guerrilla army. "Fidel was putting into words things that we all felt. Our morale was strong."

In three months, half the island was listening to Radio Rebelde. By winter, the rebels turned the popular tide against Batista.

Radio Rebelde drew volunteers to the Sierra Maestra and won supporters in the major cities.

The guerrillas, whose ranks had swelled, could now challenge Batista on the plains and in the cities. And they did. The overwhelming majority of Cuba wanted revolution. City after city fell to the rebels.

When Guevara marched troops to the key city of Santa Clara on December 28, 1958, peasant crowds cheered. Residents used overturned cars to create makeshift barricades that blocked the advance of Batista's armored vehicles, and citizens within the city threw Molotov cocktails at the defending army from the inside. Batista soldiers defected to join Guevara midfight, saying they were tired of fighting their own people. Batista was practically defeated before Guevara's troops arrived.

Within hours of his thorough defeat at Santa Clara, Batista had fled the country. On New Year's Day 1959, the rebels marched triumphantly into Havana and Fidel Castro declared Cuba free.

Revolutions are a slow, deadly business. Before radio, 300 outcasts hiding in the jungle could not have overthrown a powerful military dictatorship. But with radio, those outcasts could connect to the 5 million oppressed Cuban citizens who secretly shared the rebellion's dissatisfaction, and turn the tide against the dictator, tanks and planes and all. The radio had superconnected the revolutionaries with the Cuban people, and together they achieved victory in astonishingly short time.

THE CLASSIC MYTH OF Guevara and the Cuban revolution is that it was the pirate radio itself that helped the rebels win. But that's not the whole story. Radios don't come with built-in fan bases. Uneducated farmers generally won't put their lives in some foreigner's hands just because he says to on the radio.

Tapping networks is not as easy as simply shouting a message. Guevara became a successful superconnector not because he broadcast, but because he managed to build a relationship with the people.

This chapter, and the third lever of this book, is about his formula for doing so.

II.

The guy who makes *Star Wars* movies for a living works out of a three-story building in Santa Monica, California, that bears the moniker "National Typewriter Company."

No, it's not George Lucas, and the guy doesn't actually make typewriters; he just likes them. His company is actually called Bad Robot Productions, and the tiny wooden plaque on the charcoal door to the left of the typewriter sign—next to the door with no handle and above the keypad with the glowing green button—reads, "Are you ready?"

I was ready. But I didn't make it inside that door. Reports from those who have indicate that the office beyond is full of eclectic sci-fi artwork and a bookshelf that opens to reveal a secret toilet. The middle-aged man in business attire who approached me from outside after I knocked said that, "The typewriter repair shop isn't open to public," but I was welcome to check out the website, nationaltypewriters.com. I peeked beyond the door when he used his key to slip inside, and it certainly wasn't a typewriter shop.

I'd been e-mailing with the Bad Robot people earlier and they'd tried to shield me from this place, and from the man behind the company: Jeffrey Jacob Abrams, the recently tapped director of *Star Wars VII*.

Born in New York City, with a Super 8 film camera already

in his infant arms, Abrams had spent his entire life wanting to make movies. By his early 40s, he'd become one of the most successful and sought-after directors in the business, and possibly the most powerful man in sci-fi since Steven Spielberg. Abrams had created the hit TV shows *Alias* and *Lost*, directed *Mission Impossible* and *Star Trek* films, and made a movie with Spielberg himself. And now, Abrams had been anointed heir to George Lucas's legacy, meanwhile launching and maintaining a dozen other high-profile directorial projects.

But before all that, like most artists, Abrams struggled to get his first break.

He wrote nine screenplays that went nowhere. "I think each one was worse than the one before it," he once told author Steven Priggé. "I couldn't do it." Then he ran into a writer friend, Jill Mazursky, whose father was a well-connected movie director. Abrams proposed that Mazursky and he cowrite a script and that she work her father's network to get it into some high-profile hands. The plan worked, and Abrams's first screenplay became *Taking Care of Business*, starring Jim Belushi.

This is the classic Hollywood networking story: make friends with people who have connections and work them to your advantage. Be nice to them when you need them, then move on.

When we look at Abrams's subsequent film credits, we can see that the method worked well for him. He collaborated with bigger and better writers and directors and actors, from Harrison Ford to Michael Bay, and used their credibility (Sinatra style) and networks to work his way up the Hollywood chain.

But then something curious happened. The self-serving Hollywood networking theory starts to break down when we look at Abrams's credits from *after* he became wildly successful; it turns out that even once he was on top, he continued to *co*write, *co*direct, and *co*create almost *all* his projects. He started lending his own Sinatra-style credibility to less known but talented writers and directors and actors, so they could climb their ladders faster.

Dr. Adam Grant, professor of organizational psychology at the Wharton School of the University of Pennsylvania, says this is because J. J. Abrams is "a giver," a rarity in an industry full of takers. No good TV show or film is made by one person, but whereas Hollywood bigshots are known for being credit-hogs, J. J. Abrams is a fantastic collaborator.

Grant would know. He wrote the book on the subject. In his bestseller, *Give and Take*, he presents rigorous research showing that a disproportionate number of the most successful people in a given industry are extremely generous. From medical students to engineers to salespeople, his studies find givers at the top of the ladder.

"Being a giver doesn't require extraordinary acts of sacrifice," Grant writes in *Give and Take*. "It just involves a focus on acting in the interests of others, such as by giving help, providing mentoring, sharing credit, or making connections for others."

Abrams is known, acquaintances tell me, for his kindness and lack of ego, in addition to his penchant for mystery. That's how he attracts the best people to his staff. And that's how he's managed to climb so far so fast.* Staffers with whom I e-mailed and met at the "typewriter shop" were eager to keep Abrams away from me because, according to his reputation, he'd probably spend way too much time helping this shaggy-haired writer out when he ought to be, you know, filming *Star Wars*.

Initially, Abrams helped out better-connected people than himself, and doing so helped him superconnect. But once *he* was the superconnector, he still helped people. That's how to tell if someone is a giver, or a taker in giver's clothing. "If you do it only to succeed," Grant says, in the long run, "it probably won't work."

---

* Though we have to give Abrams credit for being a memorable storyteller, too.

Sonny Moore, from chapter 5, leveraged this concept of helping better-connected artists and accelerated his own success. A peculiar culture of remixing and collaborating with other DJs became a strong element of the electronic dance music scene in Los Angeles in the late 2000s, and when Sonny remixed artists like Lady Gaga or Avicii or Nero, he gave their tracks a boost and helped them reach new fans. This in turn superconnected Moore to audiences larger than his own and led to surges in his popularity. And after winning six Grammys, Moore started paying things forward, incubating new and young artists in his recording warehouse and promoting their music to his fans.

Jack Canfield, from chapter 2, similarly superconnected into networks when he released his book, *Chicken Soup for the Pet Lover's Soul.* He partnered with a national pet supply retailer to offer a half-price coupon for the book to anyone who bought a 50-pound bag of dog food. The company promoted the deal across the United States. "The principle was partner up with somebody who is already a gorilla, that has huge reach and impact, and create a win-win," Canfield explains. Eager for a deal, dog owners bought half a million books—and in the process, a lot of dog food. It was one of the fastest book launches of Canfield's career.

"The number one problem with networking is people are out for themselves," says Scott Gerber, founder of the Young Entrepreneur Council, who coined the term *superconnector.* "Superconnecting is about learning what people need, then talking about 'how do we create something of value.'"

This is a twist on the classic networking advice, which advocates boldly meeting people and asking them for things. Building relationships through giving is more work than begging for help, but it's also much more powerful.

And there's a simple way that companies can do it, too. . . .

III.

In 2006 a Silicon Valley engineer named Aaron Patzer quit his job to start a company called Mint Software, Inc., an online service that helped people simplify their personal finances. Mint users could collect all their bank accounts and credit card information in one place and track their spending and savings with nice charts. Mint would then suggest ways to save money, such as by transferring balances to credit cards with lower rates (at which point the company received a commission).

At the time, the convention was for startups like Mint to acquire users by spending heavily on advertising. But Mint tried something different.

Instead of interrupting people with ads, Mint decided it was going to become a media company that taught people to better understand finances. It started a blog on which it posted helpful articles about money management and savings. The blog chugged along, slowly winning audience members to its free content, and then it found a way to tap into a large broadcast channel: social bookmarking.

Social bookmarking sites were all the rage in the mid-2000s. Here people shared links to content they liked, while others "voted" on which links they liked best. The highest voted stories every day surfaced to the front pages of bookmarking giants like Digg.com and Reddit.com, where millions of people saw them.

So Mint started making blog posts its editors thought were likely to be voted up by the bookmarking crowds. Its editors commissioned infographics* (illustrated stories that made sense of data) explaining economic trends in terms a normal person could

---

* Full disclosure: I freelanced as a designer and writer for Mint during this time.

understand. These were entertaining, informative, and visually striking stories, and they helped people grasp money management in a fun and noncondescending way.

Some of the most influential Digg and Reddit users fell in love with the Mint blog, which gave them content that would make them look good to their own fans. Those influential users shared these stories, sending millions of visitors to Mint.com.

Thus Mint built relationships with an enormous number of people—by helping them. Over the next two years, 1.5 million people who discovered Mint through its blog posts ended up actually signing up for Mint's service. In 2009 Patzer sold the business to Intuit for $170 million.

Mystic energy isn't the secret to the success of Grant's givers; just as we learn from Mint, when we give and teach, we build up fan bases that become more likely to support us.

And that, actually, was the key component of Che and Fidel's revolution.

IV.

When Che Guevara began broadcasting Radio Rebelde's revolutionary message into Cuba's villages, the locals didn't instantaneously rise up to join the cause. If Fulgencio Batista's regime provided one thing, it was predictability. Yes, the people were oppressed. Yes, the poor starved and the mob ran amok. But as history has repeatedly shown, people with lives and families tend to favor predictability even in the worst of circumstances. Revolution would probably mean deaths—all the worse if the rebels lost—and surely the upending of what meager livelihoods many peasants already struggled to cling on to. If you were uneducated, illiterate, and barely surviving, leaving your job and family to fight for "the greater good" would seem highly irrational, wouldn't it? That job and family might not be there when you returned, and then what?

"Radio Rebelde truly became our means of mass communication, to talk to the people," Castro later recalled. But he and his crew knew that talk was not enough to win the people to the cause. Their countrymen's basic needs had to be met, and trust had to be gained.

So, Guevara started teaching peasants how to read. The revolutionaries, largely an educated bunch, walked into villages and set up classes. They taught the poor how to farm, how to be self-sufficient. They taught them self-defense. The villagers began to see the rebels as their allies—people actively improving their immediate circumstances. The rebels' service spoke much louder than Batista's pompous speeches.

Radio Rebelde became a tool for reinforcing that service, for teaching and inspiring during the day, and reporting the news at night.

Guevara was adamant that everything Radio Rebelde broadcast be 100 percent true. Batista used radio to spread lies about false victories and impress people with his supposed power, but he was a taker. The lies caught up to him as rebels detailed the destructions of military convoys and revealed troop movements and inventories; they reported the news, and the regime was frequently embarrassed.

"The radio should be ruled by the fundamental principle of popular propaganda, which is truth," Guevara later wrote. "It is preferable to tell the truth, small in its dimensions, than a large lie artfully embellished." He knew that if his message was honest, he'd win the hearts of the people in the long run.

And, unsurprisingly, a strong relationship developed between the rebels and the proletariat. Castro's movement earned the citizens' trust. And then together they took back their country.

Despite the ensuing decades of tension between the United States and Cuba, and despite Cuba's stagnant economics, Cuba's literacy rate is 99.8 percent today, putting it in the top ten countries in the world (and slightly above the United States). And although Fidel has turned out to be a less-giving ruler than a younger version of himself might have hoped, the octogenarian Castro's approval rating in Cuba remains higher than the percentage of Americans who approve of their own Congress.* Che, true to his giving self, eventually headed off to Congo and Bolivia to teach them and join their freedom fights.

In the end, Castro's revolutionary message reached a massive audience through a superconnector—a radio—but the rebels won the people's hearts because they showed that they sincerely cared. The movement harnessed the power of the superconnector by giving service as a publisher and educator. J. J. Abrams built his career by collaborating with talented, fast-rising, and well-connected people and by making them look great. And Mint grew business via its own broadcast on the Web, tapping super-connected people and then helping the members of those people's networks through meaningful content.

No matter the medium or method, giving is the timeless smart-cut for harnessing superconnectors and creating serendipity.

What happens post-serendipity—as we'll learn in the final part of this book—is where things start to get really interesting.

---

* Sadly, that's not hard to beat at the time of this writing. A 2013 poll found that the 112th Congress was less popular than cockroaches, root canals, lice, carnies, colonoscopies, and Nickelback.

PART III

SOAR

Why fit in when you were born to stand out?

— Dr. Seuss (attributed)

Chapter 7

MOMENTUM

"Depressed Billionaires"

I.

In January 2010 Paul "Bear" Vasquez, a burly, cheerful man who lived just outside of Yosemite National Park in central California, posted a home video to the website YouTube. A handful of people saw it.

Six months later, late-night television host Jimmy Kimmel discovered the clip and shared it on Twitter, calling it "the funniest video in the world."

A fad ignited. Kimmel's fans watched and shared, and the dormant video instantly shot to 1 million views. Within two weeks, it hit 5 million. Kimmel invited Vasquez to appear on his show, further boosting the video's exposure. Suddenly the video was being spoofed on Cartoon Network and *College Humor*, parodied by Jimmy Fallon and indie musician Amanda Palmer, and auto-tuned by the infamous Internet comedians the Gregory Brothers.

If you had an Internet connection and lived in North America at the time, you may have seen it. Vasquez is the man behind the "Double Rainbow" video, which at last check had 38 million views. In the clip, Vasquez pans his camera back and forth to show twin rainbows he'd discovered outside his house, first whispering in awe, then escalating in volume and emotion as he's swept away in the moment. He hoots with delight, monologues about the rainbows' beauty, sobs, and eventually waxes existential.

"What does it mean?" Vasquez crows into the camera toward the end of the clip, voice filled with tears of sheer joy, marveling at rainbows like no man ever has or probably ever will again. It's hard to watch without cracking up.

That same month, the viral blog *BuzzFeed* boosted a different YouTuber's visibility. Michelle Phan, a 23-year-old Vietnamese American makeup artist, posted a home video tutorial about how to apply makeup to re-create music star Lady Gaga's look from the recently popular music video "Bad Romance." *BuzzFeed* gushed, its followers shared, and Lady Gaga's massive fanbase caught wind of the young Asian girl who taught you how to transform into Gaga.

Once again, the Internet took the video and ran with it. Phan's clip eventually clocked in at roughly the same number of views as "Double Rainbow."

These two YouTube sensations shared a spotlight in the same summer. Tens of millions of people watched them, because of a couple of superconnectors.

So where are Vasquez and Phan now?

Bear Vasquez has posted more than 1,300 videos now, inspired by the runaway success of "Double Rainbow." But most of them have been completely ignored. After Kimmel and the subsequent media flurry, Vasquez spent the next few years trying to recapture the magic—and inadvertent comedy—of that moment. But his monologues about wild turkeys or clips of himself swimming in lakes just don't seem to find their way to the chuckling masses like "Double Rainbow" did. He sells "Double Rainbow" T-shirts. And wears them.

Today, Michelle Phan is widely considered the cosmetic queen of the Internet, and is the second-most-watched female YouTuber in the world. Her videos have a collective 800 million views. She amassed 5 million YouTube subscribers, and became the official video makeup artist for Lancôme, one of the largest cosmetics brands in the world. Phan has since founded the beauty-sample delivery company Ipsy.com, which has more than 150,000 paying subscribers, and created her own line of L'Oréal cosmetics. She continues to run her video business—now a full-blown production company—which has brought in millions of dollars from advertising. She's shot to the top of a hypercompetitive industry at an improbably young age. And she's still climbing.

Bear Vasquez is still cheerful. But he's not been able to capitalize on his one-time success. Michelle Phan could be the next Estée Lauder.

This chapter is about what she did differently.

II.

In the late 1990s, the Internet created thousands of millionaires— and a handful of billionaires—in Silicon Valley. Many entrepreneurs who rode the wave early and bailed out before it crashed in the early aughts suddenly found themselves in an unfamiliar position: having worked 80-hour weeks at Internet startups for the past few years, they now no longer needed to work at all. *Ever.* For the millionaires, smart financial planning meant a comfortable life and the freedom to pursue new things. For the billionaires, champagne baths every morning and new Lamborghinis every afternoon couldn't deplete the fathomless amount of cash on hand. "Your entire philosophy of money changes," writes author Richard Frank in his book, *Richistan.* "You realize that you can't possibly spend all of your fortune, or even part of it, in your lifetime, and that your money will probably grow over the years even if you spend lavishly."

There are dotcom entrepreneurs who could live top 1 percent American lifestyles and not run out of cash for 4,000 years. People who Bill Simmons would call "pajama rich," so rich they can go to a five-star restaurant or sit courtside at the NBA playoffs in their pajamas. They have so much money that they have nothing to prove to anyone.

And many of them are totally depressed.

You'll remember the anecdote I shared in this book's introduction about being too short to reach between the Olympic rings at the playground jungle gym. I had to jump to grab the first ring and then swing like a pendulum in order to reach the next ring. To get to the third ring, I had to use the momentum from the previous swing to keep going. If I held on to the previous ring too long, I'd stop and wouldn't be able to get enough speed to reach the next ring.

This is Isaac Newton's first law of motion at work: objects in motion tend to stay in motion, unless acted on by external forces. Once you start swinging, it's easier to keep swinging than to slow down.

The problem with some rapid success, it turns out, is that lucky breaks like Bear Vasquez's YouTube success or an entrepreneur cashing out on an Internet wave are like having someone lift you up so you can grab one of the Olympic rings. Even if you get dropped off somewhere far along the chain, you're stuck in one spot.

Financial planners say that this is why a surprisingly high percentage of the rapidly wealthy get depressed. As therapist Manfred Kets de Vries once put it in an interview with *The Telegraph*, "When money is available in near-limitless quantities, the victim sinks into a kind of inertia."

Wait—the victim? We're calling the courtside pajama guy a victim?

It's hard to feel entirely sorry for him, but in a sense, yes. Life has stopped moving forward. When businesspeople cash out big, says wealth coach Susan Bradley, "Momentum has been building for a while. Then there's this moment that it's over, and all the champagne is gone, and there's this feeling of this drop into an abyss. It's like the beams of a house have gone away and you have to build from the inside out. That sense is paralyzing. It actually affects our cognitive functioning."

I'm pretty sure that acquiring a billion dollars would solve all my problems. However, studies show that the wealthy—especially those who fall into it through inheritance or the lottery or sale of a business—are often *not* happier once they're rich. A meaningful percentage of them believe that their wealth causes more problems than it solves.

If you want to get really depressed about success, look at what happened to the heroic astronauts of the 1960s and '70s. Buzz Aldrin, the second man to set foot on the moon, returned home from the historic *Apollo 11* mission and became an alcoholic. Severely depressed, his life unraveled. Aldrin burned through three marriages and wrote two memoirs about his misery. Neil Armstrong, the man who stepped out of *Apollo 11* just ahead of Aldrin, spent his next few decades figuring out what to do with his life. He briefly taught some small classes at a university, then quit unexpectedly. He consulted a little for NASA and some random companies, and did a commercial for Chrysler, and quit all those things, too. He hid from autograph seekers and sued companies for using his name in ads.

There were certainly multiple factors contributing to these men's post-moonwalk slump, but the question *What do you do after walking on the moon?* became a gigantic speed bump.

The trouble with moonwalkers and billionaires is when they arrive at the top, their momentum often stops. If they don't manage to find something to parlay, they turn into the kid on the jungle gym who just hangs from the ring.

Not coincidentally, this is the same reason that only one-third of Americans are happy at their jobs. When there's no forward momentum in our careers, we get depressed, too.

As Newton pointed out, *an object at rest tends to stay at rest.*

So how does one avoid billionaire's depression? Or regular person's stuck-in-a-dead-end-job, lack-of-momentum-fueled depression?

Harvard Business School professor Teresa Amabile took on the question in the mid-2000s in a research study of white-collar employees. She tasked 238 pencil pushers in various industries to keep daily work diaries. The workers answered open-ended questions about how they felt, what events in their days stood out. Amabile and her fellow researchers then dissected the 12,000 resulting entries, searching for patterns in what affects people's "inner" work lives the most dramatically.

The answer, it turned out, is simply progress. A sense of forward motion. *Regardless how small.*

And that's the interesting part. Amabile found that minor victories at work were nearly as psychologically powerful as major breakthroughs. To motivate stuck employees, as Amabile and her colleague Steven J. Kramer suggest in their book, *The Progress Principle*, businesses need to help their workers experience lots of tiny wins. (And as we learned from the bored BYU students in chapter 1, breaking up big challenges into tiny ones also *speeds up* progress.)

This is helpful to know when motivating employees. But it also hints at what billionaires and astronauts can do to stave off the depression that follows the high of getting to the top.

To get out of the funk, say Joan DiFuria and Stephen Goldbart, cofounders of the Money, Meaning & Choices Institute, depressed successes simply have to start the Olympic rings over. Some use their money to create new businesses. Others parlay sideways and get into philanthropy. And others simply pick up hobbies that take time to master. Even if the subsequent endeavors are smaller than their previous ones, the depression dissipates as they make progress.

They don't have to do something Bigger or Better to be happy. They just have to keep moving.

Not every astronaut struggled postspace like Buzz Aldrin did. Several parlayed sideways rather than stopping their momentum. Earth orbiter John Glenn went into politics. Alan Shepard, America's first man in space and the fifth to stand on the moon, became a successful businessman. Alan Bean, who moonwalked in the *Apollo 12* mission, became a painter. And *Apollo 15* spaceman James Irwin found fulfillment in helping others as a minister. Each parlayed his momentum into something that kept the wheels of life turning.

Happy astronauts catch waves that lead to the moon, and then use the momentum to switch ladders to fulfilling careers on earth. Depression-avoidant entrepreneurs use levers to get massively rich, then parlay the momentum to build more things. But when Bear Vasquez tried to parlay his momentum for more, he got nowhere.

What did he do wrong?

III.

I hope you'll indulge me for a moment while I describe one of my favorite indulgences. It's a cookie: two layers of textured chocolate with a layer of confectionery cream between them. Alone, the cookie is fine, but when dunked into milk, it's magic. I can eat ten in one sitting. In fact, before I realized that metabolism is exhaustible (at some point in my twenties), I routinely ate entire packages of them.

I'm talking, of course, about the Oreo, the sandwich cookie created in 1912 that one (albeit rather dubious) study claims is as addictive as cocaine. My intense affection for Oreos went a bit stale, however, in the winter of 2013, when all of a sudden, the entire advertising industry started talking about Oreos and refused to shut up.

It was February 3, and the Baltimore Ravens were facing the San Francisco 49ers in America's most televised event of the year, the Super Bowl. Seventy-three thousand fans screamed from the bleachers of the Mercedes-Benz Superdome in New Orleans, while millions more screamed from couches around the country. For two hours, several large, sweaty men crashed into each other on a big patch of grass. Baltimore managed to score 28 points to San Francisco's 6 by the third quarter. And then, without warning, the Superdome lights went out.

Maintenance crews and stadium officials scrambled to get the power back on while players, coaches, fans, and couch potatoes waited in the dark for 34 minutes.

During the blackout, the Twitter user @Oreo sent a status update. A picture of a dark room lit up by a solitary cookie. Caption: *You can still dunk in the dark.*

Fifteen thousand Super Bowl fans, with nothing else to do while they waited for the game to resume, retweeted, or shared, @Oreo's picture. Another 20,000 fans "Liked" it on Facebook. And then the lights came back on, and one of the teams of sweaty men beat the other one.

@Oreo's tweet was clever. It was the most popular tweet of the event, in fact. But for perspective, 35,000 people is only three hundredths of 1 percent of the 108.69 million people who watched the Super Bowl. "Dunk in the Dark" was dramatically outviewed by every one of the television advertisements that aired during commercial breaks.

And yet.

Months later that Oreo tweet, now chiseled into the stone tablets of history as *the* Oreo tweet, received a truckload of awards and trophies, including two Clios. Not because the ad was amazingly designed. And not because more potential Oreo buyers saw the tweet versus Oreo's Super Bowl TV commercial. But because Oreo managed to harness momentum with it and smother the insular advertising industry with its story.

The momentum started when the tech blogs caught wind of the tweet. On game day, *BuzzFeed* wrote about the tweet in a post that earned 400,000 views. CNET and a handful of others wrote as well. The next day, *Mashable* posted an article titled, "Someone Give This Oreo Employee a Raise." That story itself was also likely viewed more times than the actual tweet.

Then the *Chicago Tribune* and *Washington Post* wrote about it. *Advertising Age* and *Adweek* wrote about how everyone else was writing about it. The frenzy of media coverage resulted in what Oreo's advertising agency, 360i, claims were 525 million earned media impressions. ("Earned media impressions" is one of those inflated figures agencies tend to use to gauge how many people *could have seen* something—akin to counting every car that drives by a billboard on the interstate—but 525 million is still a *lot*.)

Hardly anyone saw the tweet itself, but an enormous number of people heard about it later. And people within the advertising and PR industries didn't stop hearing about it.

On the surface, the Oreo tweet's incredible velocity looked like a modern runaway carriage. A corporate version of "Double Rainbow." It wasn't until I sat down as a guest judge for Digiday's digital advertising awards that I discovered the underlying story.

As the other judges and I rifled through submissions from various agencies hoping to be considered for the best advertising of the year, we came across a self-nomination from 360i, arguing that

Oreo be considered for the category of best creative. The application boasted about the press coverage the Oreo tweet had received. "*Wired* magazine declared Oreo as the Super Bowl winner, and *Adweek* even ranked the tweet as one of the top five 'ads' of the night," 360i wrote.

The agency was invoking Frank Sinatra, leaning on the credibility of bigger and better press and awards in order to parlay for even more awards. Upon inspection, it turns out this was exactly what the agency had done from the moment it sent the tweet. Fifteen thousand retweets is nothing to sneeze at, but our friend Justin Bieber from chapter 2 gets more tweets when he sneezes. (In fact, that same February 3, Bieber received 17,000 retweets for his tweet of, "chill day. off to nyc soon for SNL week!") But a trade blogger doesn't necessarily know or care about that. As soon as the Oreo tweet received some traction, 360i folks e-mailed bloggers the stats. When the blogs wrote, the agency made sure the growing story worked its way up the chain to bigger writers and publications, continuing to escalate things by making all the press coverage (earned media impressions) the story, rather than the relatively low number of Twitter shares. And so on, until the Cannes International Film Festival handed 360i a Silver Lion, and I, the ten-Oreos-at-a-time guy, felt I had to deliver an impassioned speech to the other Digiday judges about how that picture of an Oreo cookie on a black background was actually pretty run-of-the-mill creative work.

Didn't matter. Oreo's momentum had already taken it into orbit. My fellow judges voted Oreo the winner. I threw my hands up, then bought a pack of Oreos to console myself.

MOMENTUM ISN'T JUST A powerful ingredient of success. It's also a powerful predictor of success.

Eric Paley, a successful entrepreneur (he sold his dental imaging company, Brontes, for $95 million in 2006) and managing partner of the venture capital fund Founder Collective,* illustrates how this principle works in finance. A few years ago, two of his companies went out to raise money from new investors. They were in the same general industry and had the exact same economics. Each company received offers from investors around the same time, wherein the investors determined how "valuable" each business was.

Below are the basic financials for each company. See if you can guess which got a better deal:

COMPANY A
- Year 1 revenues $12M, operating at a $2M loss.
- Year 2 revenues $20M, operating at breakeven.

COMPANY B
- Year 1 revenues $6M, operating at a $2M loss.
- Year 2 revenues $20M, operating at breakeven.

Though they were both operating at breakeven with the same revenues, investors valued Company B at *double* the price of Company A, simply because Company B had more momentum.

Investors see momentum and future success as so highly correlated that they will take bigger bets on companies with fast-growing user bases even if the companies are bleeding money.

Momentum, it turns out, can cover a multitude of sins.

3601 HAD BEEN CLEVER to direct the award judges' attention away from the Oreo tweet's absolute economics and toward the *momentum* the tweet had in the press. And rather than cross

---

* Full disclosure: Paley is one of my own investors.

their fingers like many of us would, 360i's publicists had taken the tweet's initial momentum and pushed it along like sweepers in a curling match.

If 360i hadn't kept swinging, it certainly would not have won all those Clios.

The Oreo tweet case study proves that the *perception* of momentum is often as good as momentum. I didn't personally believe it deserved all the attention it got. And yet, here I am, perpetuating the Oreo tweet even further. That's the power of momentum.

Now the question is how can we manufacture—and harness—momentum that no one can argue with?

IV.

Michelle Phan grew up in California with her Vietnamese parents. The classic American immigrant story of the impoverished but hardworking parents who toil to create a better life for the next generation was marred, in Phan's case, by her father's gambling addiction. The Phan clan moved from city to city, state to state, downsizing and recapitalizing and dodging creditors and downsizing some more. Eventually, Phan found herself sleeping on a hard floor, age 16, living with her mother, who earned rent money as a nail salon worker and bought groceries with food stamps.

Throughout primary and secondary school, Phan escaped from her problems through art. She loved to watch *PBS*, where painter Bob Ross calmly drew happy little trees. "He made everything so positive," Phan recalls. "If you wanted to learn how to paint, and you wanted to also calm down and have a therapeutic session at home, you watched Bob Ross."

She started drawing and painting herself, often using the notes pages in the back of the telephone book as her canvas. And, imitating Ross, she started making tutorials for her friends and posting them on her blog. Drawing, making Halloween costumes, applying cosmetics—the topic didn't matter.

For three years, she blogged her problems away, fancying herself an amateur teacher of her peers and gaining a modest teenage following. This and odd jobs were her life, until a kind uncle gave her mother a few thousand dollars to buy furniture, which was used instead to send Phan to Ringling College of Art and Design.

Prepared to study hard and survive on a shoestring, Phan, on her first day at Ringling, encountered a street team which was handing out free MacBook laptops, complete with front-facing webcams, from an anonymous donor. Phan later told me, with moist eyes, "If I had not gotten that laptop, I wouldn't be here today."

With the webcam—and a portable computer powerful enough to edit video—she parlayed the blog for a YouTube channel, where Phan made her tutorials visual. She filmed herself applying artistic makeup while smiling into the camera, then edited the footage and added Ross-style voiceovers to explain what she was doing.

In 2007 she recorded six makeup tutorial videos. She filmed them in her tiny bathroom. Each received modest views—often in the low thousands. In 2008 Phan recorded six more. Then in 2009 when YouTube announced a program to help artists make a living from their videos, she recorded 54. Phan grew a small but loyal audience. She worked as a waitress at a sushi joint to make ends meet and recorded videos in her spare time, hoping to make some money from advertising.

That same year, 2009, Lady Gaga released her now-iconic "Bad Romance" music video. It quickly became YouTube's most-watched. Phan decided to capitalize on the wave by posting a tutorial of how to re-create Gaga's makeup from the video.

Then, like Oreo, she tried to manufacture some momentum. Like a surfer arriving hours before a competition to watch the waves, "I would study the algorithm of YouTube's front page" for months, Phan says. "I noticed that they only would post up videos with a lot of views [on the home page], and you only have 2 days to capitalize off of all these views." However, YouTube didn't update the home page on weekends, she realized. If she managed to get a video on there on a Thursday, "I [could] be there for an extra 2 days."

So she uploaded her Gaga video at the optimal moment and then notified her little group of fans to watch it at once. It was enough to reach the home page. This was the tiny nudge that got the snowball rolling. And, as the video hung on the homepage for those extra days, a writer from *BuzzFeed* noticed it and wrote a story about it.

Readers swarmed over to YouTube to watch it.

This is the part where most lucky breakers, like Bear Vasquez, would enjoy the ride until the momentum dissipated.

But instead of fading away after the fad was over, something else happened to Phan's momentum: the people who watched the Lady Gaga tutorial started watching Phan's *other* tutorials— which were excellent. Her unknown older work benefited from the spillover. Scores of the *BuzzFeed* viewers subscribed to Phan's channel, eager for more videos. Phan upgraded her camera and started recording.

Phan's backlog of content allowed her to take the momentum caused by waves and superconnectors and *capture* it. Those viewers became hers. When she posted more videos, they kept her swinging from ring to ring. And by constantly feeding them with great new content, she transformed her video series into a career and a company.

"Most YouTubers just kind of drop off around a certain time; it's hard to keep that momentum," Phan says. "I [had] to strike while the iron's hot."

AS WE'VE LEARNED FROM Michelle Phan's story, the secret to harnessing momentum is to build up potential energy, so that unexpected opportunities can be amplified. On the playground, it's like building a tower to stand on, so you can start your Olympic ring with more velocity. Phan's tower was a backlog of quality content. This is how innovators like Sal Khan (who published 1,000 math lessons online before being discovered by Bill Gates, who thrust him into the spotlight and propelled him to build a groundbreaking digital school called Khan Academy), and musicians like Rodriguez (a folk singer whose amazing, but largely unrecognized music work from the 1970s was featured in a 2012 documentary, which then catapulted him to world fame) became "overnight" successes. None of them *were* overnight successes. But each of their backlogs became reservoirs, ready to become torrents as soon as the dam was removed.

Then there's Oreo.

The untold portion of the Oreo tweet story, the part that most of the salivating bloggers missed, is what 360i and Oreo did *before* the Super Bowl. For six months, Oreo had been posting culturally relevant images like "Dunk in the Dark" on Twitter *every day of the week*. It had slowly built up a following. In the process, Oreo had honed its publishing process, which for big companies was not nearly as simple as writing 140 characters and pressing "Tweet." This was at a time when social media managers at Fortune 500 companies typically had to brave a phalanx of corporate approvers to publish anything.*

While building its content backlog, Oreo managed to get its

---

* A typical lead time for a tweet was often over a week. In an extreme case, a large life insurance company told my firm in 2013 that it would take 12 months to approve a blog post and that the lawyers would be suggesting edits via fax.

tweet approval process down to a few minutes' time—just enough time to say, "You can still dunk in the dark" before the Superdome lights came back on—and to grow a following among consumers and press that could kick-start momentum when the company needed it. And *that* is what won 360i its Cannes and Clios.

PAUL VASQUEZ WASN'T TRYING to make a funny viral video when he filmed "Double Rainbow." He hadn't intended to become famous overnight. His video backlog consisted of random home videos of things he'd seen in his yard. When the Internet's millions barreled down his virtual street, Vasquez was caught staring into the headlights. So, he made a few bucks from advertisements, got to be on TV, and stopped at the second set of Olympic rings, where the superconnectors deposited him.

Michelle Phan, on the other hand, spent years building up potential energy. She worked hard to hone her craft, stealing from the master tutorialist Bob Ross, studying the wave patterns of YouTube's homepage, and superconnecting with media companies and the fans of famous pop icons by giving and teaching. She hacked the ladder from blogger to YouTube star to makeup spokesperson to cosmetics designer to entrepreneur.

The 30-million-view Lady Gaga tutorial was not Phan's first great video, but it was her inflection point. She had been winding up for a big swing for a long time.

"Success is like a lightning bolt," Phan once declared in an interview with *Mashable*. "It'll strike you when you least expect it, and you just have to keep the momentum going."

Chapter 8

SIMPLICITY

"Hot Babes and Paradise"

I.

Save the world wasn't in Jane Chen's five-year plan when she landed an enviable consultant position at Monitor Group right out of college. But three years in, she read a *New York Times* article that changed that.

The story was about a ghastly AIDS epidemic in China. "A switch went off in my head," the Taiwanese-descended California native said. "I could just as easily have been born there."

Chen realized, "I had won the genetic lottery."

She quit the job and joined a nonprofit. She traveled and saw how the destitute half of the world lived. Eventually, she ended up at Stanford Business School studying "Design for Extreme Afford-ability," or how to create products for people who live on less than a dollar a day.

That's when she found out about the babies.

At the time, 20 million premature or low-weight infants entered the world every year. Most of them were born in developing countries. In the first world, a one-kilogram baby could be nursed to full health in an incubator in a hospital's neonatal intensive care unit (NICU). However, in poor nations like India and Pakistan (the two accounted for more than a quarter of the world's preterm births), most mothers had access to no such care. Millions of their babies didn't make it through the first year of life.

Worst of all, the World Health Organization estimated that three-quarters of those deaths could be prevented with proper equipment.

Infant life-support tech had come a long way by the time Chen found out about the babies, in 2008. In the 1800s some physicians recommended incubating preterm infants in warm crates, but it wasn't until after World War II that more sophisticated incubation equipment became a feature of many US hospitals. Inspired in part by chicken-egg incubators, hospitals began placing the fragile infants in clear, heated boxes, where they could be kept warm and sterile. By the 1970s most developed-world hospitals had NICUs with glass incubators. The survival rate of babies born weighing less than 1.5 kilograms shot from 40 to 80 percent. Incubators went from what looked like china cabinets to six-by-two-by-three-foot, space-age plastic pods with easy-access arm ports (for minimal heat loss when handling the infant) and built-in life support—ventilators and cardiorespiratory monitors and the like. Every iteration of the incubator was bigger and better than the last. After fifty years of improvements, NICU tech had gotten pricey. The typical incubator cost between $20,000 and $40,000. Not including electricity.

At Stanford, Chen and three colleagues, an engineer, a computer scientist, and a PhD candidate studying artificial intelligence, took up the challenge to lower that cost.

"We started making a cheaper glass box," said Rahul Panicker, the AI guy, in an interview with the *Times of India*. With a little ingenuity, the team thought it could shave off some materials and electricity costs inherent to building and running a typical incubator. But components like the life-support monitors were not about to get less expensive anytime soon. Furthermore, the team realized that the typical NICU incubator required serious training to operate. The unfortunate mothers of premature babies were often illiterate. "What was needed was not just low cost but something that [the moms could use themselves]," Chen said.

"We realized something was wrong," added Naganand Murty, the engineer, "and asked ourselves: do we need a cheaper glass box or something that will save babies' lives?"

CHEN'S TEAM STEPPED BACK to reassess its approach. *What features did the babies actually need to survive?* they pondered.

The answer, they discovered, was primarily just *warmth.* NICUs kept premature babies nice and toasty. Sure, they kept the kids clean and sterile, too, and they kept track of heart rate and respiration and other things. But many—Chen says most—premature infant mortalities involved complications arising from simply being too cold. (Premature babies are born with too little fat, which they need to stay warm while their bodies develop outside of the mother's womb.) The other features of the incubators made a difference in only a tiny percentage of cases, Chen says. To prevent the majority of preterm infant deaths, her team realized, they just needed to figure out how to keep a baby at a constant 98.6 degrees. And *that* was something you ought to be able to do for less than $20,000.

From that realization came Embrace, which Chen describes as, "a sleeping bag for babies." It's a tight, insulated pouch with two compartments: one for the baby and one for a hot pad that's heated in a small box—something like a toaster.

It worked. The tight enclosure kept the baby's own body heat from escaping. The bag's insulation and hot pad regulated temperature at 98.6, and the pad lasted four to six hours on a 30-minute charge. The most uneducated mother in the world could figure it out, and it kept underweight babies alive and developing.

Perhaps most miraculous, however, was the cost at which they could produce each unit: $25. One thousand times less than the cost of a NICU incubator.

Chen and her colleagues moved to India. They field tested Embrace, improving it over dozens of iterations. They created a nonprofit organization to give the Embrace away for free to mothers who couldn't afford it, and later added a for-profit arm to the company to sell the warmers inexpensively to hospitals that could.

In January 2013 Chen told me, "We've saved 3,000 babies so far." By that September, Embrace reported that the number of preterm infants protected by the Embrace warmer had increased to 39,000. Embrace won design awards, grants, and venture investments. The team grew. Chen suddenly became a spokeswoman for developing-world health issues, and even first-world hospitals started calling about the warmer.

Thirty-nine thousand infants with a fighting chance of living a normal life is incredible. But Embrace's story is just beginning. The last time I spoke with Chen, she said, "Our goal is to get these for every baby in the world."

SOMETIMES BIGGER IS NOT better. Sometimes more of a good thing is too much. Sometimes the smartest next step is a step back.

In the case of neonatal incubators, incrementally bigger and more powerful improvements meant, at the very most, incrementally less expensive (though it was usually the opposite). The hacker's approach to NICU design was to think smaller. In doing so, Chen's team created something world class.

This teaches us something important about breakthrough

success: *simplification* often makes the difference between good and amazing.

Let's step back for a moment and talk about *innovation*. Over the last several years, we've bastardized the word. Today, we equate it with change or general improvement, a buzzword meaning "bigger" or a synonym for *creative*. But the word used to mean "upheaval" or "transformation." It comes from the Latin *innovare*, *in* meaning "into" and *novus* meaning "new"; the word *innovate* in Middle English meant to "renew" or "refresh." Innovation is about doing something differently, rather than creating something from nothing (invention) or doing the same thing better (improvement). Harvard management professor Clayton M. Christensen furthered this concept in the mid-'90s when he coined the term "disruptive innovation." Disruptive innovation is when the introduction of a lower-cost product steals market share from existing players, like when e-mail usurped postal mail (how much would you spend a month if every e-mail cost the price of a postage stamp?) or when Craigslist replaced costly classified newspaper ads with free Internet listings.

The key feature of disruptively innovative products is cost savings (either time or money). But the key ingredient behind the scenes of every disruptive product is simplification. E-mail is not just cheaper, but simpler than postal mail. USB flash drives were not just less expensive than compact discs, but simpler to use. And cloud storage became even simpler than flash. Automobiles won out over horse-and-carriage because they made transportation simpler. The machines themselves were complicated, but Henry Ford kept the complexity under the Model T's hood.

There are a lot of great inventors and improvers in the world. But those who hack world-class success tend to be the ones who can focus relentlessly on a tiny number of things. In other words, to soar, we need to simplify.

- - - - - -

TECH WRITER BRIAN LAM, known to friends as Blam, was one of the first to give me a shot as a journalist. In his early career, he worked both smart and hard, parlaying from photocopying intern at *Wired* to editor in chief of *Gizmodo*, Gawker's popular gadget blog. He took the blog from 13 million to 180 million page views per month during his five-year tenure. Blam pioneered a new style of tech blogging, consistently scooped mainstream media, and made Gawker CEO Nick Denton a lot of money.

But he also gained 30 pounds, and was, as he tells me, "an angry boss and boyfriend and pretty miserable."

The next rung on Blam's ladder was not a prestigious job at *CNN* or the *New York Times*, as one might expect. (He had plenty of such offers.) Instead, he moved to Hawaii to become a surf bum.

Well, not just a surf bum. He leveraged his *Gizmodo* cred (Frank Sinatra style!) to launch a small website called *TheWirecutter*, a gadget-review site that takes simplicity seriously.

If you want to know which type of wireless speakers to buy, a typical blog—or store—will show you scads of options. Brands. Versions. Specs. Upgrades. Pros and cons. Features! Benefits! STRESS!

Blam will simply tell you that Logitech's UE Mini Boom speakers are the best.

And then he'll go surfing. Rather than worrying about inventories and shipping and cost-of-goods-sold and all the other headaches of a typical electronics business, his website sends you to Amazon. When you buy those Mini Boom speakers there (as I recently did), *TheWirecutter* gets a small kickback.

With simplified costs and no full-time employees, Blam was soon working one day a week, living in paradise, and making more money than he ever did at *Gizmodo*.

Most important, he was a lot happier.

OFTEN, THE THING HOLDING us back from success is our inability to say no. Think back to the Olympic rings analogy. We can't keep the momentum going if we don't let go of the ring behind us as we swing forward. By breaking that weakness and simplifying, Blam became untethered, able to move on to better things.

In a wonderful scene in Sir Arthur Conan Doyle's *A Study in Scarlet*, detective Sherlock Holmes chides his companion, Dr. Watson, for explaining to him that the earth revolves around the sun, which Holmes previously did not know.

"Now that I do know it I shall do my best to forget it," Holmes declared to the astonished Watson, a lifelong man of science.

"But the Solar System!" protested Watson.

"What the deuce is it to me?" said Holmes. "You say that we go round the sun. If we went round the moon it would not make a pennyworth of difference to me or to my work."

Holmes was a first-class noticer. The police leveraged him as the highest platform, if you will, in criminal profiling. His legendary powers of observation and deduction earned him the distinction of Britain's finest criminal investigator. He got to be the best by focusing on what he needed to know, knowing how to figure out what he didn't know, and forgetting about everything else.

Like Holmes, hackers strip the unnecessary from their lives. They zero in on what matters. Like great writers, innovators have the fortitude to cut the adverbs.

This is why Apple founder Steve Jobs's closet was filled with dozens of identical black turtlenecks and Levi's 501 jeans—to simplify his choices. US presidents do the same thing. "You'll see I wear only gray or blue suits," President Barack Obama told Michael Lewis for his October 2012 *Vanity Fair* cover story. "I don't want to make decisions about what I'm eating or wearing. Because I have too many other decisions to make."

I don't want to make decisions about what I'm eating or wearing? How could that possibly make one better at governing? Or problem solving? And isn't variety the very spice of life? What about creativity? Or not going crazy?

What he's talking about has been proven in experiments led by Dr. Kathleen Vohs of the University of Minnesota, experiments that show that making lots of tiny choices depletes one's subsequent self-control. Students who were forced to decide between products for long periods of time had significantly less willpower afterward than classmates who answered random questions instead. Vohs had batches of kids make choices, then do things they didn't want to do, like practice homework or drink vinegar water or hold their arms in ice water. Those who hadn't just spent time making decisions performed several times better than those who did. Apparently, patience and willpower, even creativity, are exhaustible resources. That's why so many busy and powerful people practice mind-clearing meditation and stick to rigid daily routines: to minimize distractions and maximize good decision making.

Simplification is why Steve Jobs's Magic Mouse doubled Apple's mouse market share overnight. With zero buttons (the whole thing is a button, actually) and a touchscreen glass top, the mouse is both pretty and intuitive—a huge departure from the conventional "innovative" mouse arms race, which amounted to adding more bulk and more buttons. Similarly, Apple's iPod won the MP3 player war with breakthrough simplicity, both in physical design and how the company explained it. While other companies touted "4 Gigabytes and a 0.5 Gigahertz processor!" Apple simply said, "1,000 songs in your pocket."

Constraints like that in Jane Chen's "Design for Extreme

Affordability" challenge are often the forcing functions that lead to breakthrough innovation. No one had thought to create a radically simple incubator because no one had been tasked with making one for people who live on one dollar a day. Convention said incubators were large and cost thousands, so the expected "innovation" route would have been to find cheaper plastics or optimize the assembly to inch down costs. But constraints meant Chen's team had to throw convention out. And they came up with something *more* creative than if they'd had an unlimited budget.

Here's a fact: Creativity comes easier within constraints. For example, what if I asked you to do the following exercise:

Say something funny.

Most of us freeze at such a broad challenge. Sure, there's a lot of "freedom" in it, but somehow it's tough to come up with something on the spot. Now, say I put a constraint on the exercise:

Tell me a knock-knock joke.

For most of us, this one's much easier. There's a formula to follow. You can probably think of a few right away. And if you're coming up with a joke from scratch, the knock-knock is going to be significantly easier.

Constraints make the haiku one of the world's most moving poetic forms. They give us boundaries that direct our focus and allow us to be *more* creative. This is, coincidentally, why tiny startup companies frequently come up with breakthrough ideas. They start with so few resources that they're forced to come up with simplifying solutions.

Constraints made New York City an architectural marvel. Manhattan Island's narrow shape forced the city to build up, to rethink and renew; it impelled architects to reinvent stone buildings into steel skyscrapers.

Remember Tony Wagner and the Finland phenomenon from chapter 4? Finland's education system built a higher platform—a better starting point—for its students by requiring all teachers to have master's degrees and deep expertise in *teaching how to learn.* That was half of Wagner's explanation for Finland's rapid ascent to educational greatness. The second half had to do with what the Finns *didn't* do. Over the decades, Finnish education, in fact, had gotten simpler. Instead of teaching kids a little about a lot of things—like most schools do—the Finns started teaching deeply in fewer subjects. Rather than emphasizing general knowledge students would promptly forget, they cut filler and taught vocational skills.

"Less is more" and "small is beautiful" are common aphorisms in Finland, and Finnish schools injected them into the curriculum. While every other country added more tests, more homework, and more athletics—with decreasing academic results—Finland scaled back on all of the above.

"Walk into the typical high school in America. What do you see? The first thing you see? A wall full of trophies. Are they academic trophies? Hell no. They are athletic trophies," Wagner says. "We don't celebrate academic achievements," Wagner says. "We celebrate athleticism, and I think it's sending all the wrong messages to kids."

In Finland, on the other hand, there are no school sports teams. As sad as that may sound to those of us who grew up cheering on the football team, the lack of in-school athletics allowed Finland to focus minds and resources and sprint forward *academically.* Kids can play intramural sports on their own and on the weekends, but they go to school to learn.

Classes were small, yes. But more interestingly, students often had the same teachers for several years in a row, developing rapport and allowing teachers to focus heavily on individual students' needs.

Students start learning vocations like engineering and business as soon as they hit high school. They skip many of the general education courses most of us forget. And they actually *like* school.

Research shows that kids who are tenaciously focused—psychologist Angela Duckworth calls them "gritty"—beat smarter kids in spelling bees. Their hard practice is targeted, simplified. This is the art of being a first-class *focuser.*

Geniuses and presidents strip meaningless choices from their day, so they can simplify their lives and think. Inventors and entrepreneurs ask, *How could we make this product simpler?* The answer transforms good to incredible.

Perhaps that's why Steve Jobs referred to simplicity as "the ultimate sophistication."

Holmes, on the other hand, would simply call it *elementary.*

Chapter 9

10X THINKING

"The Rocketeer"

I.

On a pleasant Sunday evening in August 2008 three hundred scientists gathered to watch their handiwork leave earth.

Their handiwork was a 70-foot rocket called *Falcon 1*. It stood tall on Omelek Island, a solitary spot of rock roughly 2,500 miles southwest of Honolulu. The 7.9-acre island that had formerly operated as the Ronald Reagan Ballistic Missile Defense Test Site now served as launch pad for a private company called SpaceX. The scientists, a colorful mob of T-shirts and polos, gazed at the island and at their missile from across the world, in a white-walled workshop at 1 Rocket Road in Hawthorne, California.

Falcon 1 was to be the first nongovernment spacecraft to orbit the planet. If the day's launch went as planned, the name of the company, printed in dark, futuristic letters on *Falcon 1*'s side, would be etched into record books and documentaries alongside *Sputnik* and *Apollo*. It would be a historic victory for the new space age.

That is, if it didn't fall dead into the ocean like the first two *Falcon*s.

Sixteen months had passed since the previous *Falcon 1* hadn't quite made it to orbit. After liftoff, the first stage (or bottom half) of the rocket successfully separated, falling to earth to allow the second stage (the rest of the rocket) to shoot into orbit. But the second stage engine unexpectedly shut off after seven and a half minutes. SpaceX engineers diagnosed the trouble and spent the next year working around the clock to perfect and polish every rivet. Now they milled about in the high-ceilinged corporate command room, abuzz with excitement. This could be it. As they waited beneath the giant screens broadcasting their rocket's video feed from 4,955 miles away, the man behind their mission stepped into the mission control trailer at the back of the room.

Elon Musk. The dark-haired South African entered, wearing his usual outfit—fitted T-shirt and jeans—and took command. The oft-mythologized billionaire—after whom Robert Downey Jr. modeled his character, Tony Stark, in the *Iron Man* films—was at the time simply a millionaire and perhaps not even that. Into SpaceX he'd plunged his personal fortune, which over six years had been whittled down to a stump.

A few years ago, Musk had disclosed that he had enough money to attempt three rocket launches. He regretted saying it. Now, after two unsuccessful attempts to reach orbit, the eyes of his 300 exhausted employees, many of whom had worked 80-hour weeks during the summer, stared at the *Falcon 1* video feed. And so did thousands of spectators around the globe.

ELON MUSK GREW UP in Pretoria, South Africa, in a family of five whose patriarch left when the kids were young. The young Elon preferred books to sports, and he was always making things. Around age ten, he ran out of books, so he read the encyclopedia, "out of desperation," he says. At age twelve, he programmed a space-battle video game and sold it. At sixteen, he tried to open a video arcade, but he couldn't get government permission to use the location he'd picked. He kept reading books.

By age 31 he was living in California and had sold two successful companies. The second, the online payments company PayPal, made him $165 million.

When a friend asked him what he wanted to do next, Musk remarked that he'd always been interested in space. "I didn't think there was anything I could do as an individual. But," he told *Wired* magazine in 2012, "it seemed clear that we would send people to Mars." That excited him. It would be an important step for humanity—he was convinced. However, when he checked NASA's website, he found no Mars mission.

It turned out that in a 1989 study, NASA had estimated a half-trillion-dollar price tag on a manned trip to Mars. Since then, politicians wouldn't touch the idea.

Musk was piqued. He had built two businesses in an industry ruled by Moore's law, the principle that says technology gets exponentially cheaper and more powerful over time. *Space flight ought to be getting easier*, he thought. Perhaps he could use his Internet money and expertise to nudge the industry forward.

So he bought some books.*

In the six ensuing years, Musk became one of the world's foremost experts on rocketry. He hunted down mavericks like aerospace consultant Jim Cantrell, who helped him put together an *Ocean's Eleven*–like team of rocket scientists. "I thought he was a lunatic," Cantrell recalls. But Musk's plan was too tempting to turn down.

Cantrell took the gig. And they started building spaceships.

---

* Musk loves biographies and autobiographies. (Serial inventor Ben Franklin's are his favorite.) But in this case, he bought books on rocket science.

— — — — —

WHEN SPACEX LAUNCHED IN 2002, NASA employed about 18,000 people and many more contractors. About 400,000 people had contributed to the Apollo program, according to author Catherine Thimmesh, who years later tallied up all the spacesuit seamstresses and propulsion engineers and software experts involved.

Musk's vision was to do with a tiny team what NASA wouldn't with its tens of thousands: "To make life multiplanetary," he said, as often as he had occasion to talk about it. To ensure the continuation of "human consciousness."

There was a problem, however. Space is expensive.

"If I were asked what were the ten most important tasks that need to be accomplished to enable a vibrant, expansive future in space for humanity, I would put lowering the cost of getting to space for all ten," says Clark Lindsey, researcher and managing editor of *NewSpace Watch*.

Since the 1950s government-funded rocketry had focused on performance—getting the most stuff into orbit as possible—with very little effort to reduce cost. The average Space Shuttle mission, for example, cost over $1 billion, all told. *Every time.* As such, NASA had effectively abandoned the idea of manned flight to Mars, suggesting that maybe in the late 2030s it might—possibly, almost, perhaps, hopefully, our-fingers-are-crossed, but-don't-hold-us-to-it—think about it.

SpaceX's goal of getting to Mars would mean necessarily reducing the cost per kilogram of stuff launched into space from thousands of dollars to tens of dollars.

Early on SpaceX discovered that most aerospace contractors sold parts at sky-high, gouge-the-government prices. A lot of R&D goes into the development of the various components used in rocket engines, so companies like Lockheed and Boeing charged a premium for them, even though the parts themselves didn't cost much to make—sort of like drugmakers do with medication. Musk figured a first-class noticer could build those components himself—a generic acetaminophen to Boeing's Tylenol—and perhaps even improve upon them.

Musk built a factory designed to input aluminum and spit out rocket parts. Rather than paying NASA prices for engine nozzles and manifolds and heat shields, SpaceX manufactured its own at a fraction of the cost. The happy side-benefit of this was greater control over inventory, as aerospace delivery times for parts from manufacturers were notoriously bad.

Next, Musk sought simplification. He reduced complexity by making the various stages of his rocket the same diameter, with the same engines. Whereas most rockets used fuel tanks of diminishing fatness (the Shuttle, for example, had two small boosters and one big booster, which required different tools, parts, and procedures to build and maintain), *Falcon*'s two stages could be built with the same jigs and tooling, the same electronics, and the same engineers.

The strategy lowered costs, says Musk, "by at least a factor of two, and perhaps as much as three or four compared to similar vehicles elsewhere. This came despite the conventional wisdom in the space industry, academia, etc., that rocket costs couldn't be reduced by more than a few percent."

That's great, except the *Falcon* had already failed twice. So much for cost savings. Before he could go to Mars, Musk had to prove he could put something into space at all.

As Musk's third and final rocket's engines warmed up half a world away on Omelek Island, an electric feeling filled the cavernous room at SpaceX headquarters. The gathered scientists stared at the screens, "like a couple hundred people against the world," remembers SpaceX head of talent Dolly Singh. Inside *Falcon 1*'s belly rested a payload of three small satellites and the ashes of actor James Doohan, the actor who played Scotty in the original *Star Trek* series. And the last pennies of Elon Musk's fortune.

As Musk watched the countdown in his command trailer at the back of the building, his bank account hovering near zero and 300 of his friends' six years of sacrifice having led up to this one moment, his heart must have raced.

This has to work.

II.

At first, nobody seemed to take SpaceX seriously. This was an Internet millionaire playing with his money. That's what the insular, good ol' boys club of rocket contractors told everyone. And Musk wasn't the first newbie in history to think he could take on space. "There's a long list of people who've tried to do this," Cantrell says. "Nobody succeeds. Ever."

Musk realized that in order to gain support for his big vision, he would himself have to step into the public spotlight. In other words, he had to get people to *believe*. So the geek brushed up on speaking skills and started talking big. *This-is-the-future-of-mankind* big. He did television appearances and magazine interviews. He told the world he was going to die on Mars.

Musk isn't the first in history to use over-the-top demonstration to create buzz, and therefore harnessable momentum. Pop star Lady Gaga gained unprecedented support for her music and mission to "foster a more accepting society" through the stir generated by her outrageous costumes and music videos. Being hoisted into the 2011 Grammy Awards inside a giant egg, then hatching on stage wasn't eccentricism, it was brilliant marketing. Twenty-four million albums later, it's clear such artistic brinkmanship worked. Energy-drink maker Red Bull spurred enormous word-of-mouth when it sent daredevil Felix Baumgartner to the edge of space in a balloon, then recorded his supersonic freefall. His skydive broke the record for first human body to break the speed of sound, and the highest freefall distance (127,852 feet). Creating your own wave and then catching it is as old as ancient Greece: Alexander III rallied the Macedonians with his hyperbolic quest to reach the "ends of the world and the Great Outer Sea," conquering the entire Persian Empire along the way.

Of course, such spotlight-snatching only produces real momentum if there's substance behind it. Gaga's music was catchy and fresh. Red Bull had spent years publishing a backlog of high-octane sports content (and selling a popular beverage); the attention from Baumgartner's jump just solidified the company's reputation in the action-sports world. Alexander earned himself the title "Great" through his ingenious military tactics, without which his quest would have never worked.

President John F. Kennedy described the opportunity inherent in high-profile swings like these when he declared in September 1962 that the United States would put a man on the moon. "We choose to go to the moon in this decade and do the other things, not because they are easy, but because they are hard. Because that goal will serve to organize and measure the best of our energies and skills."

And that, at last, brings us to our final smartcut.

III.

Inside the bowels of the SpaceX factory, a kid named Kosta Grammatis, one of the youngest avionics systems engineers in the company, sat tinkering with a tiny satellite for the year leading up to the third *Falcon 1* launch. It was called K-SAT. It was basically a modem. With it, Grammatis's team hoped to use preexisting satellite networks to control SpaceX spacecraft. Essentially, hooking in to an existing platform that could save the company time and money.

After nearly failing out of high school and college, Grammatis had hacked the ladder to his position at SpaceX on the back of what he called "an epically large project," wherein he sent balloons and sensors up into the atmosphere to sniff for pesticide residue. He did it by shunning his classes (there was no physics program at the college he managed to get into) and reading a lot of articles on the Internet. He was a smart kid, a practitioner of David Heinemeier Hansson's selective slacking, and, it turns out, good at engineering.

But designing minisatellites wasn't big enough for Grammatis. After leaving SpaceX in 2009, he would go on to create a bionic eye that *Time* magazine would name one of the "world's best inventions." Even then, he wanted to do something bigger.

"A lot of people start companies and say, 'Hey, I'm gonna make a billion dollars,' and that's fine," Grammatis told me. "I'm gonna connect the entire human race to the internet."

In 2010 only 2 billion of earth's 7 billion people had Internet access. "The Internet taught me nearly everything I know," Grammatis wrote in a personal manifesto. "It is the modern-day equivalent of the library of Alexandria, except it's much harder to burn to the ground. It is indispensible for realizing human rights, combating inequality, accelerating development, and quickening the pace of human progress." He theorized that information access would be the fastest route to world peace.

With that grandiose mission, he launched AHumanRight.org, a nonprofit. In its first two years, his team successfully convinced a telecom company to move an undersea fiber-optic cable to provide

Internet access to 4,000 people on the island of Saint Helena and raised thousands of dollars toward the mission of buying a satellite from a troubled company and repositioning it over Africa to provide free Internet. The fund-raiser gained enough publicity to prove that people cared about the cause, and by 2014 Grammatis and his team had rallied the United Nations and various other organizations to help distribute satellite tablet computers—the world's first—to the world's largest refugee camp, in Dadaab, Kenya. Free Internet access would be provided by satellite owners he'd worked with in his "Buy This Satellite" campaign.

If you think "I'm gonna connect the entire human race to the Internet" sounds crazy, you're right. When you realize that he may have already done it for half a million people before age 30, Grammatis's story becomes a mini case study of the smartcut that makes Elon Musk world class.

It's called "10x Thinking."

10x Thinking is the art of the extremely big swing. To use a baseball analogy: instead of trying to get on base—or even aiming for a home run—it's trying to hit the ball into the next town.

No amount of weight lifting or swing practice will get you there. Such a goal requires you to think radically different.

The apostle of 10x Thinking is a man with perhaps the coolest name ever: Astro Teller. Teller is the goatee-and-ponytailed head of a rather secret Google laboratory in California called Google[x]. He holds a PhD in artificial intelligence.

Teller's job is to dream big. 10x big. Google's founders have endowed him with an engineer-filled building and a mandate to blow their minds. His team has built self-driving cars, augmented reality glasses, and WiFi balloons meant to roam the stratosphere. He's hired some brilliant minds onto his team, but that's not the secret of their success.

The secret sounds a bit crazy. Says Teller, "It's often *easier* to make something 10 times better than it is to make it 10 percent better."

Hmm. Math would seem to suggest otherwise. Let's let the man named Astro explain himself:

"The way of going about trying to make something new or better often tends to polarize into one of two styles," Teller says. "One is the low-variance, no surprises version of improvement. The production model, if you will. You tend to get '10 percent,' in order of magnitude, kind of improvements."

"In order to get really big improvements, you usually have to start over in one or more ways. You have to break some of the basic assumptions and, of course, you can't know ahead of time. It's by definition counterintuitive."

Incremental progress, he says, depends on working harder. More resources, more effort. 10x progress is built on bravery and creativity instead. Working smarter.

In other words, 10x goals *force* you to come up with smartcuts.

"I joke that this is a moon-shot factory," Teller says, of Google[x]. "Our belief is that if you can get people to let go of their fear, and to be more intellectually open, intellectually honest, more dispassionate about being creative, trying new things, and then being honest about what the results are instead of having all these other issues cloud their judgment, you can get to radically better solutions in honestly about the same amount of time, about the same amount of resources, as making the 10-percent improvement."

Elon Musk calls this "getting to first principles." In the 1800s 10 percent style thinking for faster personal transportation translated into trying to breed stronger horses. First principles would suggest instead thinking about the physics of forward movement, then building up from there, leveraging the latest technology—like the internal combustion engine.

Most "innovation" inside industries and companies today focuses on making faster horses, not automobiles. That's why so many of us fall victim to the innovator's dilemma, wherein competitors usurp while we think we're being innovative.

First principles force us to let go of paradigms. "You can trade in a ton of effort in exchange for just the right perspective," Teller says. He uses the analogy of trying to shoot an arrow through an orchard. "You could shoot an awful lot of arrows trying to get all the way through the orchard. But the really, the best thing to do would be to move around until you got the trees lined up. That process of not spending all of your time shooting the arrows, but trying to reframe the problem . . . is really about bravery, about creativity."

But wait, are we just building a case for 10x-style swings based on the word of billionaire-funded crazy people?

Academic research actually shows that we're less likely to perform at our peak potential when we're reaching for low-hanging fruit. That's in part because there's more competition at the bottom of the tree than at the top. And competition in large numbers doesn't just decrease general odds of winning. It creates underperformance.

In 2009 behavioral psychologists Stephen M. Garcia and Avishalom Tor showed that merely knowing there are more competitors in a competition decreases our performance. Not relative to a group, but in *absolute* terms.

They call this the N-Effect. To prove it, Garcia and Tor had students take competitive tests, some with only ten people taking the test, others with 100. Over and over, they changed the variables of the experiment: the students took the test in the same room or they took them alone, but they knew others were taking it too. Without fail, the students competing in smaller clusters scored higher. At a certain point, adding more competitors dampened the effect (if you're competing against a thousand kids or ten thousand, it doesn't make much of a difference), but with few competitors, students pushed themselves harder, without even realizing it.

The N-Effect has been confirmed in other settings as well, such as standardized tests like the SAT and ACT. And while it's more difficult to conduct controlled experiments for it in business, businesspeople will tell you that the presence of one or two serious rivals is incredibly motivating. When the rivals number in the thousands, it's a different type of game.

Of course, some people are completely able to block social comparison out. But in general, humans are good at seeking the easy path and are deeply affected by our social surroundings at a subconscious level. The "high-hanging fruit" approach, the big swing, is more technically challenging than going after low-hanging fruit, but the diminished number of competitors in the upper branches (not to mention the necessary expertise of those that make it that high) provides fuel for 10x Thinking, and brings out our potential.

Perhaps more interesting, however, is the business research on companies that aim high philosophically. Executive Jim Stengel, formerly global marketing head of Procter & Gamble, teamed up with research firm Millward Brown in the 2000s to collect a decade's worth of data on the market performance of major brands that orient themselves around a noble purpose or ideal.

What he found was more dramatic than he expected. Brands with lofty purposes beyond making profits wildly outperformed the S&P 500. From 2001 to 2011, an investment in the 50 most idealistic brands—the ones opting for the high-hanging purpose and not just low-hanging profits—would have been 400 percent more profitable than shares of an S&P index fund.

Why is this? The simple explanation is that human nature makes us surprisingly willing to support big ideals and big swings.

That means more customers, more investors, and more word-of-mouth for the dreamers.

So there's evidence both in business and academia to support 10x Thinking. But not every big dream gains followers or comes true. Just because you're righteous doesn't mean people will support you. You have to motivate them. You have to tell provocative stories.

This explains brands like Red Bull and Whole Foods that manage to convey their values so loudly; they tell good stories. This explains Gaga, Alexander, and other revolutionary types; they tell *fantastic* stories. This explains the furor of support that coalesced around Dr. Martin Luther King Jr. during the American civil rights movement. King stood up against the backdrop of decades of freedom fighting and painted a picture that people could believe in.

That's how we got civil rights. And that's how we got to the moon. King and Kennedy weren't simply cowboys, riding off toward some impossible goal. These were smart people, working and preaching desperately hard for what they believed in. People who realized that striving toward a massive goal and rallying people around a rethinking of life's rules and expectations and conventions were actually easier than working for small change.

"We need a movement," Kosta says, to make 10x happen. "You need to get a critical mass of people who give a fuck."

Or, as Musk likes to say, "The first step is to establish that something is possible; then probability will occur."

With 10x Thinking, Elon Musk had built a space company. Like JFK, Musk believed that the fact that it was hard was why it was going to work.

The countdown clock marched down to T minus 10 seconds. An idling cloud of white smoke wafted from the base of the rocket.

9. Kosta's precious K-SAT sat snug, inside *Falcon 1*'s belly, as the verbal countdown began.

8 . . .

7 . . .

6. The palms beside the launch pad stirred in the South Pacific breeze.

5 . . .

4 . . .

3. The engine sequence began.

2. Exhaust billowed from beneath the rocket.

1 . . .

Ignition.

Orange flame enveloped the launch pad, as it hissed from the rocket. For two seconds, *Falcon* sat motionless. Then, slowly, the 61,000-lb missile eased itself off the pad, fire gushing from its base. It roared into the air. The SpaceX team cheered. Fourteen kilometers it climbed, reaching a speed of 450 meters per second. Two and a half minutes later, *Falcon* was ready to drop its first stage engine and blast its second stage into orbit—right on schedule. With a click, the rocket separated in two and the discarded first stage tube fell away.

And the video feed cut out.

IV.

The thing about giant swings is they come with increased odds of failure. Babe Ruth swung big and smashed every home run record in baseball. He also held the record for strikeouts.

Falcon 1 crashed into itself. When the first stage fell away from the rocket, a tiny bit of fuel remained in its tank. Suddenly, the engine kicked in again. The depleted piece of rocket rear-ended the second stage, sending it, like its predecessors, into the Pacific Ocean.

The SpaceX team on the factory floor didn't know this yet. But they knew something was wrong. For several minutes, the black screens stayed black. Mission Control's trailer door remained shut. The members of the press who watched on site murmured.

As the minutes crept by, the emotional state among the SpaceX crew went from jittery to depressed. The ticking clock confirmed the worst. Years of work suddenly weighed down on the team, many of whom had worked through physical and mental exhaustion since the beginning of the company. "It felt like a funeral," Singh recalls. "It was like a patient on the operating table that dies in front of your eyes."

Finally, the trailer door opened. Out came Musk. He marched past the press, without acknowledgement, and faced his 300 colleagues.

The man who friends describe as "100 brains inside one head," who "ummed" and "ahhed" and bobbed when giving impromptu speeches, spoke clearly and resolutely.

We knew this was going to be hard, he said. *It's rocket science.* Few countries had even made it this far—and many had tried.

Then the surprise: this third launch would not be SpaceX's last.

Squaring his shoulders before his audience, Musk announced that *Falcon 1* had some secret insurance. That month, he said, he had arranged for an investment from his old colleagues at PayPal that would get SpaceX two more rockets. They would learn what had happened tonight and they would use that knowledge to make a better rocket. And they would use that better rocket to make even better rockets. And those rockets would one day take man to Mars.

"For my part," he said, "I will never give up. And I mean never."

In an instant, the dark mood flipped. The crew went from despair to excitement. From loss to resolve. They cheered, some with tears in their eyes. Musk had turned the failure into feedback.

"Elon walked out with a set of [defibrillator] paddles and was like, 'Don't die on me yet!' " Singh says. "He galvanized people in their lowest of lows."

"He just simply doesn't believe in failure," Cantrell adds. "And that makes this guy special."

It was an easy fix. A launch failure typically took NASA or others six months to figure out what happened, three months to get a new rocket out on the launch pad, and another two or three to get it certified for flight. With it's vertically integrated factory and startup spirit, SpaceX found the problem and put the next *Falcon 1* on the launchpad in five weeks.

And on September 28, 2008, it flew perfectly.*

As the first privately developed spacecraft orbited the earth for the first time in history, the triumphant SpaceX team celebrated at their favorite dive bar in nearby El Segundo. The next day, they'd be working on a bigger rocket.

Musk's big story got scientists and investors to believe. The *Falcon 1* victory got NASA to believe. In December 2008 Musk signed a $1.6 billion contract to use his rockets to start shipping supplies to the International Space Station.

In rapid succession, SpaceX parlayed the *Falcon 1* for a nine-engine *Falcon 9,* that could carry 21,000 pounds of payload and achieve orbit even if two engines failed. *Falcon 9* flawlessly flew seven times by December 2013, carrying dozens of commercial satellites at a cost of $54 million per flight—5 percent of the cost of a Space Shuttle mission.

Funding was no longer going to be a problem.

"Generally speaking, if you're gonna make something ten percent better than the way things currently are, you better be great in sales and marketing, because you're gonna have to talk people into changing

---

* See the video at shanesnow.com/falcon1.

their behavior for a very marginal increase in value," explains Astro Teller. "If, on the other hand, you make something ten times better for a large number of people—you really produce huge amounts of new value—the money's gonna come find you. Because it would be hard *not* to make money if you're really adding that much value."

This is exactly what's happened to SpaceX. As the rockets flew into space, so flew satellite orders into Musk's office. In focusing on the big vision, SpaceX built something with which it would be hard *not* to make money.

Falcon 9 paved the way to the even larger *Falcon Heavy,* and carried the Dragon capsule, which became the first private spacecraft to dock with the International Space Station. By then, SpaceX had the most powerful—and least expensive—spaceships in the world. As of this writing, the company has nearly 4,000 employees and is on course to make more rocket engines per year than the rest of the world combined. *Falcon 9 Heavy* is the most powerful aeronautic vehicle in this solar system. It can put a city bus in its cargo bay and launch it into space.

But what if SpaceX could do 10x better?

Evolutionary thinking would suggest trying to coax more thrust out of SpaceX's rockets. Revolutionary 10x Thinking might ask a more fundamental question, such as, "Why continue to make rockets that only work once?" (Or, as Musk is fond of asking, "Would America have been colonized if they had to burn the ships when they got there?")

Hence the Grasshopper, SpaceX's newest rocket at the time of this writing. Grasshopper is a *self-landing* rocket, with PICA heat shields capable of hundreds of atmospheric reentries. It launches, does its thing, and then returns, gently lowering itself back on the landing pad.

SpaceX is on its way to not just 10x, but potentially 100x decrease in the cost of getting to space.

Suddenly, Mars doesn't seem so crazy.

People are generally willing to support other people's small dreams with kind words. But we're willing to invest lives and money into huge dreams. The bigger the potential, the more people are willing to back it. That's why Musk was able to win over investors at the last moment when *Falcon 1* needed one more shot; they saw the enormous potential upside and they believed in his story.

Big causes attract big believers, big investors, big capital, big-name advisers, and big talent. They force us to rethink convention and hack the ladder of success. To engage with masters and to leverage waves and platforms and superconnectors. To swing and to simplify, to quickly turn failure into feedback. To become not just bigger, but truly better.

And they remind us, once again, that together we can achieve the implausible.

EPILOGUE

Joliet, Illinois, a neighbor of Chicago, is known to the outside world for two things: *The Blues Brothers* and a rather large prison.

The prison is now closed, but it wasn't when D'Wayne Edwards was born in Joliet in 1969. The sixth of six children to a single mom, Edwards doesn't remember much of the city, just that he was packed up and moved to someplace worse: Inglewood, California. At the time, Inglewood was known as the murder capital of the United States.

The new neighborhood was rough. Poor African American kids like the Edwardses passed time playing street ball and endured the dispiriting Inglewood public school system. Ms. Edwards worked as a nurse's assistant, but was injured on the job when Edwards was still young. The seven of them scraped by, living off of her disability assistance.

Edwards was a thoughtful kid. At Kelso Elementary School, he loved his number two pencil and showed a gift for drawing. But he kept that love a secret from the neighborhood kids. "The idea of being an artist sounds kind of sissy like—it wasn't something I talked about," he says. "I would play ball. But when I wasn't doing that, I was drawing."

The kids grew up, fatherless and floundering like so many of their peers. While his brothers experimented with cigarettes and alcohol, young Edwards began fixating on something a little lower to the ground: sneakers. By sixth grade, he was drawing shoes every day. He drew them on three-by-five index cards. "It was the perfect size to draw a shoe on," he said. He would sit a shoe down in front of him and try to copy it perfectly. He'd study the footwear of his sports heroes, like Pittsburgh Steelers running back Franco Harris, who wore PONY shoes.

All through middle school, Edwards kept sketching. His math teacher, Mrs. Weathers, often busted him drawing sneakers during class. She would take the index cards away. When he got to high school—countless sketches later—he was nudged out of art class because he was better than the teacher. The school felt it was a waste of time for him to take art and put him in drafting class instead, where he could learn some discipline. He called this lateral education "the best gift I've gotten." The drafting teacher, Mr. Petrosian, who kids called Petra, caught Edwards filling in lines by hand when he should be using rulers. Edwards had the ability to draw a straight line free hand. He explains, "I would measure something out and it would be a quarter of an inch short, and I would just free hand 'cuz it was quicker." Petra would mark him off.

By age 16, Edwards's sneaker habit was getting expensive. "I started buying shoes on my own because my mother didn't have any money to buy me the latest sneakers that I wanted." Foot Locker wouldn't hire him, so he got a job at McDonald's. "It was kind of like *Coming to America*. Like Eddie and Arsenio, I had to mop the grease on the floor." He worked his way up to burger flipper, then assistant manager.

In the 1980s Inglewood was a tough place to grow up; poor

kids dreamed of making it out of the city through sports, though precious few managed it. Many of the rest ended up dead or in jail. "My options were pretty limited," Edwards recalls. "It was either to leave the city in a bag, or go to jail, or be part of this drug gang." He saw the damage drugs did to older kids he knew, and shied away. ("To this day I don't drink or smoke," he says, " 'Cuz I saw my brothers did it.")

Adults encouraged him to hang on to the McDonald's job. Someday he might become a regional manager, they said. Edwards hated the idea. One day on his lunch break, while browsing classifieds for a new job, he saw a tiny advertisement in the *Los Angeles Times*—a quarter of an inch by an inch big—that said "Design Competition" and "Reebok" and a phone number.

It turns out that Reebok's Santa Monica office was hosting a shoe sketching contest. The prize was a job. Edwards drew several entries, made his way across town, and dropped them off. Three weeks later, he got a phone call saying he'd won.

Reebok didn't realize how young he was. When Edwards showed up to the office, the Reebok employee said, "Whoa, we can't hire a high school kid! Come back when you graduate from college." Edwards was heartbroken. He had the ability; why did his age matter? Furthermore, his family was broke; none of his siblings had gone to college. "I told Reebok, 'I'm gonna come back, but I'll make you guys regret it,'" Edwards says.

The rejection sparked a determination: *I will become a shoe designer.* He told his boss at McDonald's that he was going to prove it. She said, "No, you're not gonna do that." He went to his high school guidance counselor and asked what courses he could take to learn the sneaker trade.

She said, "Black people don't design footwear."

After he graduated from Inglewood High, art schools like Otis–Parsons were too expensive, given his meager income. So he ended up working temp jobs while studying at night at a community college.

To his delight, the temp agency placed him as a file clerk at LA Gear, a shoe brand founded in 1983 by a man named Robert Greenberg.

Day in and out, Edwards filed paperwork. But one day, the company installed suggestion boxes around the office to solicit employee feedback. One of the boxes was right by his desk. Edwards began putting his index cards into it. Every day, he dropped a new shoe sketch through the slit of that wooden box, asking for feedback on each design.

Nobody responded. But Edwards persisted.

After six months, Greenberg called Edwards into his office. On his desk was a stack of Edwards's sketches. *What school did you learn to do this at?* Greenberg asked. "I said I had no formal training," Edwards says. "I was actually just a temp."

Greenberg bought Edwards's contract from the temp agency for $1,000 and gave him a job.

Greenberg mentored Edwards personally as a designer. But another master helped Edwards overcome his obstacles in *life*. That master was a deceased baseball player.

"One day I was in the library, and I found this book on Jackie Robinson," Edwards says. "I had never heard of Jackie Robinson. When I started to read his story, it led me to the Negro Leagues. I didn't know that existed, and as I started to get into black history and sports and what Jackie had to go through, the thing that resonated with me is Jackie wasn't the most talented. They brought Jackie up because of not just his physical abilities, but his mental strength. He would have to endure more than other players would have to. He wouldn't be allowed to speak up; he had to just let his play speak for him.

"He learned more about people by observing than really talking to them. He learned more through observation. That was kind of a gift that was given to him, [and] he learned a lot more about people and a lot more about himself.

"So I learned from him. I didn't talk. I just observed," he continues. "And I worked harder than they did. And I was hungrier than they were."

Edwards had an innate sense of what the typical sneaker consumer wanted. As the '80s sneakerhead movement erupted, all these black kids on the streets were suddenly buying basketball shoes, but none of the sneaker designers had ever spent a day in those kids shoes. Except Edwards. "It made the things I designed sell well."

He did fantastic work, and was beloved by the company. By 23, he was promoted to head designer, one of the youngest in the business.

But Edwards didn't get comfortable. He moved on from LA Gear to Skechers, then Nike, where he became one of the company's youngest design directors. In his first year at Nike, he designed the brand's best-selling boot of all time (Goadome 2), which still sells nearly a million pairs each year. By age 30 he was sitting down with Michael Jordan to craft the NBA legend's signature shoe. MJ wanted the design to be inspired by his favorite car, the Bentley Continental. "I learned everything there was to know about this car. Sure enough he was pressing me, 'What about this, what about that?' Just drilling me. And I'm firing right back," Edwards recalls. "And once he knew that I did my homework, after that it just became two friends talking about sneakers, man. It was just one of those surreal moments."

Edwards became one of eight people to ever design an Air Jordan sneaker. By his mid-30s, he found himself at the very top of the footwear design industry. He designed signature shoes for Carmelo Anthony and Derek Jeter. His kicks were worn by gold medal Olympians. His designs sold more than $1 billion worth of product.

But he felt itchy. He had made amazing friends in footwear, but was bothered to see African Americans so underrepresented in the industry. "Years later, and 5,000 designers later, there were still only about 100 people of color," he says.

Midway through his career at Nike, he started going back to Inglewood. "I would go back to my old high school at least twice a year and just talk to the kids and let them know, 'I was in the same seat you were sitting in, and I was able to get out of the city—and I didn't play ball at all!' Just trying to get them to understand that if you can't play ball, it's not the end of your life."

They needed to know they could make it out of the inner city, like he had. "I just wanted to give them hope."

That was around the time Google happened. Kids around the world started posting sketches of shoes on the Internet—talented artists like young Edwards. Middle-aged Edwards started replying to their posts, giving them feedback. Sneaker junkies connected the dots and realized he was *the* D'Wayne Edwards. They craved his advice. He began mentoring kids from afar. And he suddenly realized how he could help those inner-city kids get out of Inglewood.

"I was blessed to have a platform like Jordan where people know who I am. But I could have a bigger impact at this industry," he said, "if I could design lives."

So Edwards quit his job.

He began courting shoe brands and athletes like Carmelo Anthony—whom he had mentored while at Jordan—to help him start a design contest called Future Sole, much like the Reebok contest he won in high school. He approached Nike and Adidas and proposed, "What if you have a different conversation with your consumer: instead of telling them just to run, jump, and dunk, what if you tell these kids they can be a designer?"

But the contests weren't enough. So he started PENSOLE—a portmanteau word made up of Edwards's two favorite things—which quickly became the world's most prestigious footwear design academy. A literal boot camp. Edwards harnessed the momentum of his lucrative career to rally industry support to fund and train the next generation of footwear artistes. He set up partner programs with the schools he could never afford, like Parsons the New School for Design and Art Center College of Design. He got Converse and Under Armour and Adidas and other big names in the industry to sponsor entry contests and pay the tuition for deserving students from around the world. He built diverse classrooms, and he recruited students and mentors from another underrepresented group in footwear: women.

PENSOLE's m.o. was to mimic the real-world shoe design process. In Edwards's studio in Portland—and on-site at partner schools around the United States—he gave students design briefs like, "Create a shoe using 3D printing," and taught them to do market research and build consumer profiles, sketch and design, then actually create physical shoe models out of masking tape and eventually real materials.

"I learned on the job. I teach that way," Edwards says. "I put them in the exact same position than when they're at a company."

PENSOLE students work 12 to 14 hours a day, for four to six weeks. They draw a dozen shoe sketches one day, get critical feedback, then draw ten more, whittling down and iterating until they produce real, professional-grade shoes.

"Color is a distraction. Computers are distractions," Edwards says. He forces his students to simplify, drawing concepts in pencil and then using computers and color to bring their designs to life once the architecture is perfect.

As important as the design process itself, Edwards teaches his students personal discipline and the ability to market oneself.

At PENSOLE, "They start to position themselves as if they were a brand," Edwards explains. "When you're the brand first, you approach life differently. If you're the brand, you want to protect your brand. You want to clean up what your Facebook looks like."

"One of the first things he told me was, 'you need to get yourself a network,'" says Sarah Sabino, a former student of Edwards's who now designs kids' shoes for Converse. At their first meeting, "He patted me on my back and said, 'People say it's all about who you meet, but to me it's about who you make part of your circle that really matters.'" To that end, Edwards brings in industry luminaries to personally mentor students and give inspiring talks. He connects his students to projects where they can help industry greats, and empowers those greats to give back to the next generation; many of them see that opportunity as a gift itself.

Students hardly sleep. "The days were very very intense days," says Precious Hannah, a PENSOLE student from Miami who now works at Brand Jordan. "It was way more than shoe design." By the end of the program, PENSOLE students have worked harder than they have in their lives; more important, they've learned to work *smart*.

So far, he's placed more than 70 of them in top shoe design jobs.

Jackie Robinson knew that if he didn't make it in baseball, it would be a long time before another black kid got a shot. Robert Greenberg gave Edwards that first shot. "Even to this day," Edwards says. "Many years later and many dollars later, I still have this burning desire to make sure he knows he didn't make a mistake.

"I thank him every time I see him," Edwards says. And then, unaware that his own student has just told me the same thing about Edwards himself: "In some ways he was a father figure I didn't have."

- - - - - -

IN *SMARTCUTS*, I'VE CATALOGED the patterns through which rapid successes and breakthrough innovators achieved the incredible. The nine principles comprise a framework for breaking convention that explains how many of the world's most successful people and businesses do so much with less.

D'Wayne Edwards's story fits the framework beautifully:

#1: HACKING THE LADDER

"I always wanted to be better." Edwards built his own nontraditional ladder and constantly pushed himself to climb. There was no comfortable plateau, but always a trade for something more. "I challenge my kids to be better than they were yesterday," he says. "When you look at your life in daily increments to try to succeed daily, that builds over time." It was his sideways path into shoe design that made his shoes sell so well. And, like the best presidents, it was Edwards's sideways ladder switch from the top of his industry—and the Sinatra-style credibility of having designed for Michael Jordan—that made PENSOLE successful so quickly.

#2: TRAINING WITH MASTERS

Edwards had no sneaker design mentor in the early days, so he copied his favorite shoes down on paper. He literally stole Magic Johnson's discarded shoes so he could draw and then wear them. In the process, he became a first-class noticer, a master of tiny details about how shoes are put together and how consumers on the street think about them. A decades-long relationship with his mentor Robert Greenberg helped Edwards master the shoe business, but most important, Edwards's personal relationship with the deceased Jackie Robinson guided his life's journey.

#3: RAPID FEEDBACK

For months, Edwards drew a shoe a day and asked for feedback at LA Gear. He used Reebok's rejection to push himself to become better instead of considering himself a failure. And his design process at PENSOLE is built around rapid feedback, so that students can squeeze semesters' worth of learning into a few weeks' time.

#4: PLATFORMS

Though the brands Edwards designed for became platforms from which he could spring in his own career, the most important platform was the one he built. PENSOLE allowed Edwards to scale himself, to reach, teach, finance, and place more talented kids in footwear design careers than he could before.

#5: CATCHING WAVES

Edwards rode into shoe design on a shift in consumer behavior that happened in the 1980s and '90s: the sneakerhead movement. Shoe materials were evolving, as was the design process, and athletic footwear evolved from heavy leather boots to cross-trainers and basketball pumps. During this period, poor kids who loved sports started buying—even collecting—great sneakers. "You can be completely flat broke and have a $100 pair of shoes on," Edwards said. "That will make a kid feel so good, doesn't matter if his jeans are bummy, if his jacket is his brother's." Edwards became the ideal designer for this generation because he came from the streets where the sneakers ended up. He was in the water before the wave came.

#6: SUPERCONNECTING

Along his journey, Edwards built a powerful network and a name for himself in the industry. He was able to leverage star athletes like Carmelo Anthony to promote his shoe design contest, Future Sole, and eventually his PENSOLE academy. But first, he taught and mentored those stars in how to brand themselves. Edwards superconnected his students to top designers and businesspeople, giving the industry mavens opportunities to give back and feel good, and students opportunities to contribute fresh perspectives to competitive companies. He also superconnected to top design schools, giving his curriculum and expertise to other programs, and leaning on the reputations and contact lists of Parsons, et al., to reach more potential students.

#7: MOMENTUM

PENSOLE came about on the heels of Edwards's personal momentum in the industry. He didn't start teaching because he was washed up; he left Nike when he was on top and still moving. That momentum helped him attract sponsors and supporters and launch his academy like a rocket.

#8: SIMPLICITY

Edwards cut PENSOLE's curriculum and process down to core principles. He constrained the class to just a few weeks' time in order to instill urgency and focus on what's core. There's no conventional school busywork. He made students draw initial designs in black and white and by hand in order to get them to think more creatively than they would with the crutches of color and rendering.

#9: 10X THINKING

"My mission?" Edwards chuckles. "Change education and change the industry." This huge vision gained him rabid support and forced him to teach his students more than just design, the deep life skills that they'll need to thrive in the shoe industry. And this is what makes PENSOLE special.

D'WAYNE EDWARDS USED ALL the principles of *Smartcuts* to change his and others' lives, sometimes intentionally, often not. He made his own path, found leverage to do more in less time, and swung for the fences. And now his students are paying it forward.

What we put on our feet matters. But what Edwards has done transcends footwear. More than 20 years after he started putting those index cards in the LA Gear suggestion box, he's sold all the shoes he could dream of. What matters most at the end of the day is not how many sneakers he's shipped, but how many people he's helped become a little bigger or better.

I hope we, too, can use the principles in this book to improve our lives and careers. I hope businesses use them to build great companies and create terrific products.

But I hope we can do something 10x bigger than that. What stops us from applying the principles of *Smartcuts* to macro problems? To lifting societies out of oppression and the poor out of poverty? To making each generation a little bit better than the last? To making the world a better place?

We can do incredible things by rejecting convention and working smarter. What would happen if we looked at problems like pollution and climate change, racism and classism, violence and hunger, and instead of waiting for luck to strike, asked ourselves, "How can we use smartcuts to fix things faster?"

You can make incremental progress by playing by the rules. To create breakthrough change, you have to break the rules.

Let's break some big ones together.

ACKNOWLEDGMENTS

Books are a team effort. There are too many people to thank for this one, but I'll name a few who were instrumental: Kristen, for believing in me more than I did. Jim Levine, for being the best agent an author could ask for. My editors, Hollis Heimbouch and Colleen Lawrie, for guiding everything—and for dealing with my neuroses. My business partners Joe Coleman and Dave Goldberg, for generously supporting me in this endeavor *while* building a company. Frank Morgan, Esq., for all the research, writing help, fact checking, and moral support. Brandon, for constantly saying, "I'm so excited for your book!" and Natalie, for frequently commiserating. Drew, for telling me what was boring, and Andrew, for making sure I didn't turn into a slug in the process. My fact checkers: Taylor Beck (*Fast Company*), Chuck Wilson (the *New York Times*), and Elise Craig (*Wired*), for saving me from myself. My parents, for everything. All my friends at Contently who believe in the power of great stories. Adam Bair, for getting me my first newspaper job and inspiring me to move to New York. The Starbucks on Forty-Ninth Street and Eighth Avenue, for letting me live in the corner chair for twelve months, and for all the free drinks. And to all the other teachers and friends whose names I have not space to list: my deepest gratitude. The secret word is *kangaroo*.

NOTES

INTRODUCTION: "HOW DO THEY MOVE SO FAST?"

1   *world record for the fastest completion*: The technical category in which Nathan Parkinson won the world record was "Super Mario All-Stars / NTSC–Super Mario Bros. Minimalist Speed Run." *Super Mario Bros.* as played on the Super Mario All-Stars cartridge has a few different quirks from the original NES cartridge, and there is a separate world record for each cartridge. Nate's record was verified and posted by Twin Galaxies, "World Records: Super Mario All-Stars / NTSC–Super Mario Bros. Minimalist Speed Run," http://www.twingalaxies.com/operator.php?game id=5632&platformid=32&variationid=17228 (accessed May 27, 2013).

2   *Bundled with the original Nintendo*: Super Mario Bros. was bundled with the original NES in 1986, but, intriguingly, no one knows exactly when the game first came out: Frank Cifaldi, "Sad but True: We Can't Prove When Super Mario Bros. Came Out," *Gamasutra* (blog), http:// gamasutra.com/view/feature/167392/sad_but_true_we_cant_prove_ when_.php.

2   *"world's best-selling video game"*: Guinness named *Super Mario Bros.* the best-selling video game: Guinness Book of World Records, "Best Selling Video Games," http://web.archive.org/web/20060317005503/ http://www.guinnessworldrecords.com/content_pages/record.asp?recor did=52404 (accessed February 15, 2014). However, Wii Sports overtook it in 2013 with over 80 million units sold. Nintendo, "Top Selling Software Sales Units," http://www.nintendo.co.jp/ir/en/sales/software/wii .html (accessed February 15, 2014).

2   Super Mario Bros. *has 32 levels*: For everything you ever wanted to know about *Super Mario Bros.*, check out Super Mario Wiki, "Super Mario Bros.," http://www.mariowiki.com/Super_Mario_Bros.

4   *It took the oil tycoon John D. Rockefeller*: Rockefeller's billionaire journey is well-known, but a 1994 *New York Times* story about his West 54th Street house in New York City (not far from the coffee shop where I typed most of this book) gives the history from a fun angle: Gray, Christopher, "Streetscapes/The Rockefeller City House; Pied-a-Terre off Fifth for a Parsimonious Billionaire," *New York Times*, May 22, 1994, http://www.nytimes.com/1994/05/22/realestate/streetscapes-rockefeller-city-house-pied-terre-off-fifth-for-parsimonious.html.

4   *Michael Dell achieved billionaire status*: Dell's billionaire journey is found at "Michael Dell," *Biography*, http://www.biography.com/people/michael-dell-9542199.

4   *Bill Gates in 12*: Gates was officially declared a billionaire by Forbes: "400 Richest People in America," *Forbes*, October 1987.

4   *Jerry Yang and David Filo of Yahoo*: Bloomberg News reported Filo's billionaire status on July 3, 1998: "Yahoo Founder Attains Billionaire Status," *Los Angeles Times*, http://articles.latimes.com/1998/jul/03/business/fi-329. Shortly afterward, *Time* magazine reported Yang's billionaire status on October 12, 1998: "No. 6 Jerry Yang," *Time*, http://content.time.com/time/world/article/0,8599,2044757,00.html.

4   *It took Pierre Omidyar*: Omidyar became a billionaire in 1998. "Pierre Omidyar," *Forbes*, http://www.forbes.com/profile/pierre-omidyar/.

4   *in the late 2000s*: Andrew Mason was a billionaire on paper as of Groupon's January 2011 venture financing, according to the $15 billion company valuation that was reported by Andrew Ross Sorkin and Evelyn M. Rusli, "Groupon Advances on I.P.O. That Could Value It at $15 Billion," *New York Times*, January 13, 2011, http://dealbook.nytimes.com/2011/01/13/groupon-readies-for-an-i-p-o/. Groupon was two years old as of November 2010. (The song I listened to while preparing the previous seven citations: shanesnow.com/song1.)

4   *"A serious assessment of the history of technology"*: Ray Kurzweil, "The Law of Accelerating Returns," March 7, 2001, http://www.kurzweilai.net/the-law-of-accelerating-returns (accessed February 15, 2014). A $1.7 million computer in 1990 could do 17 million "computations" per second. By 2003 a standard Dell could do 4 *billion* calculations per second and cost $1,600. Ritchie King, "The Rise of the Machines," *Popular Science*,

http://www.popsci.com/content/computing (accessed February 15, 2014).

5   *Most large businesses stop growing*: Eighty-seven percent of large businesses stop growing, according to researchers Matthew S. Olson and Derek van Bever, *Stall Points: Most Companies Stop Growing—Yours Doesn't Have To* (Yale University Press, 2009).

5   *venture capitalists pay bright people*: Peter Thiel, an early Facebook investor, founded the Thiel Foundation, which offers whiz kids investment money to build companies instead of going to college. Learn more at Thiel Fellowship, "About the Fellowship," http://www.thielfellowship.org/become-a-fellow/about-the-program/ (accessed February 15, 2014).

7   *"If any person or persons"*: James Franklin, *New-England Courant*, December 3, 1772, http://founders.archives.gov/documents/Franklin/01-01-02-0021. The Silence Dogood Letters are found reprinted in various places online, and are also contained in Benjamin Franklin, *Silence Dogood, the Busy-Body, and Early Writings* (Library of America, 2002). For an excellent discussion of Franklin's use of disguise and lateral thinking to disrupt the status quo, see William Pencak, "Representing the Eighteenth-Century World: Benjamin Franklin, Trickster." Penn State University, http://www.trinity.edu/org/tricksters/trixway/current/vol 3/vol3_1/Pencak2.htm (accessed February 15, 2014). And, of course, no volume compares with Benjamin Franklin, *The Autobiography of Benjamin Franklin*. It's available for free via Project Gutenberg at http://www.gutenberg.org/ebooks/148.

9   *You can't hang around*: I cofounded Contently, Inc., with my friends Joe Coleman and Dave Goldberg in December 2010, with the mission of building a better media world through empowering consumers, creators, and brands to tell great stories. During the time I wrote this book, we grew 400 percent in revenue; added 20,000 journalists to our talent network; and raised $9 million in venture capital to expand operations. You can read the story at shanesnow.com/contently.

10   *Want to digitize libraries*: Yes, filling out those crazy letters on Web sign-up forms helps digitize libraries of old books! "What Is Recaptcha," Google, http://www.google.com/recaptcha/learnmore (accessed February 15, 2014).

12   *The law of the lever*: The law is explained simply by Heather Hasan, *Archimedes: The Father of Mathematics* (Rosen Publishing Group, 2006), 73.

14   *Today's world record*: Scott Kessler's 5:08 speed run time is the fastest

Super Mario Bros. game played on *any* console, according to "World Records: Super Mario Bros. NTSC Minimalist Speed Run," Twin Galaxies, http://www.twingalaxies.com/operator.php?gameid=411&platformid=23&variationid=5717 (accessed May 27, 2013).

CHAPTER ONE: HACKING THE LADDER

17 *The average president of the United States takes office*: A breakdown of biographical sources and calculations of the ages, political offices held, and time spent in elected office by each US president can be found at shanesnow.com/presidents. The average age at inauguration of a US president has hovered around 55 since Abraham Lincoln. Founding Fathers and presidents before Lincoln skewed slightly older at a running average of 57 to 58. During the first 100 years of US history, congressmen's ages averaged in the 40s, crossing 50 in the mid-1800s. If you remove 69-year-old Ronald Reagan from the list (he temporarily evens the score), the average president has been younger than the average senator since 1829. The mean age of each Congress is tracked at "Average Age by Congress and Position," American Leadership Database, http://www.lifecourse.com/rdb/indicators/age.php (accessed February 15, 2014). However, in 2011 the *Wall Street Journal* created an excellent interactive infographic of the graying Congress, which displays the information in an easily consumable way and gives a hint of the evolving "game" played throughout Congress's history: Daniel N. Fehrenbach, Alex Lowe, Kurt Wilberding, and Ana Rivas, "The Capitol's Age Pyramid: A Graying Congress," *Wall Street Journal*, http://online.wsj.com/public/resources/documents/info-CONGRESS_AGES_1009.html. The average senatorial age, which crept up a few years in the last century, is brought up to the 60s by all the people who stay stuck in the Senate for several terms. Senators tend to enter at about the same time as the typical president and they stay for an average of almost 18 years. (Some, like Daniel Inouye from Hawaii, stay nearly 50!) *Slate* points out that part of the "graying" of Congress may be because in the 1800s politics was an "up or out" game, and in the years after, it's become more common to bide one's time before climbing up, or to treat a single political office as a long-term career: Brian Palmer, "Democracy or Gerontocracy?" *Slate*, January 2, 2013, http://www.slate.com/articles/news_and_politics/explainer/2013/01/average_age_of_members_of_u_s_congress_are_our_senators_and_representatives.html.

17 *Terms in the Senate*: Though legislators (senators and representatives)

and executives (presidents and vice presidents) are members of two separate branches of government, and though state and federal government offices are technically different "ladders," the individual offices within them are commonly held in the following descending hierarchy: president, vice president, governor, senator, congressman, state senator, and state representative. Doug Wead elaborates that "How most [politicians] come up" is through a predictably sequential ladder. "The traditional: State Senator, then Majority Leader of the State Senate, now a Delegate to the DNC, now I get one of these openings for Congress and lose, and now I win, and now I look for Senate."

17 *even brand-new senators*: First-time senators in the 113th Congress were already 53 years old, on average, when they started, according to Jennifer E. Manning, "Membership of the 113th Congress: A Profile," Congressional Research Service, http://www.fas.org/sgp/crs/misc/R42964.pdf (last modified January 13, 2014; accessed February 15, 2014). However, when we exclude senators who had previously been US representatives (so we're only counting senators who switched ladders from other industries), the average age increases to 56. And in the 111th Congress, the average incoming age for new senators overall was 57, according to Jennifer E. Manning, "Membership of the 111th Congress: A Profile," Congressional Research Service, https://www.senate.gov/CRSReports/crs-publish.cfm?pid=%260BL)PL%3B%3D%0A (last modified December 27, 2010; accessed February 15, 2014).

18 *youth voter turnout*: Rock the Vote polls show that 18- to 29-year-old voters actually tend to be nearly as likely to vote in congressional races as in presidential: "Nationwide Baseline," *Rock the Vote*, August 24, 2010, http://www.rockthevote.com/assets/publications/research/2010/2010-rock-the-vote-nationwide-baseline.pdf.

18 *and the* losers *in presidential elections*: The second-place finishers in presidential races are, on average, 55. Exactly the same as the winners. For a list of losing candidates, see "Also Rans: A Chronological List of Losing Presidential Candidates of the United States," Library of Congress, http://www.loc.gov/rr/print/list/060_ran_chron.html (accessed February 15, 2014). Says presidential historian Doug Wead, "Anybody who gets to that level has gone thru a similar rite of passage."

18 *Born on a farm in Texas*: For one of the best biographies of President Lyndon B. Johnson, see Doris Kearns Goodwin, *Lyndon Johnson and the American Dream* (St. Martin's Griffin, 1991).

19 *Five were never elected*: In many of this chapter's calculations, we place an emphasis on number of years in "elected office." It's important to note, however, that holding an elected office is not the only way for one to acquire political savvy. Indeed, many of our ladder-hacking presidents held political appointments (like judgeships or secretaryships) where they would have plenty of opportunity to infiltrate political circles. Even military generals like Eisenhower and Grant could be considered politicians, despite never holding elected office. As Doug Wead says, "Eisenhower had been running for President for years in the army. He succeeded in the army in exactly the way you're describing these Presidents succeed in politics." (Eisenhower climbed the military ladder sideways from lieutenant to captain to chief of staff, to commander of Allied forces in North Africa and Europe during World War II—hardly the typical upward move—to president of Columbia University for five years, to supreme allied commander in Europe.) Interestingly, it was actually Dwight's brother Milton who people thought would become a politician. "Dwight was an afterthought," Wead says. "And just a few years later, Dwight was the President."

21 *a young Canadian man*: Kyle MacDonald parlayed his paperclip-to-house story into a 310-page book: Kyle MacDonald, *One Red Paperclip: Or How an Ordinary Man Achieved His Dream with the Help of a Simple Office Supply* (Crown Archetype, 2007).

22 *"a cumulative series of bets"*: "Define:Parlay," Google, https://www .google.com/search?q=define:parlay&oq=define:parlay (accessed February 15, 2014).

22 *"By itself, one small win"*: Karl Weick, "Small Wins," *American Psychologist* (1984): 40–49.

23 *not just their rapid cycle time*: For a bonus discussion on the effect of "cycle time" on small wins and the art of parlay, check out shanesnow .com/cycletime.

23 *"It is their agility"*: Katie Hiler, "Cheetahs' Secret Weapon: A Tight Turning Radius," *New York Times*, June 12, 2013, http://www.nytimes .com/2013/06/13/science/agility-not-speed-is-cheetahs-meal-ticket-study-says.html.

23 *One of the fastest-selling*: Apple's iPhone changed the landscape for cellular phone technology with the introduction of the iPhone in 2007. By 2012 its iPhone 5 had become the fastest-selling phone in history, at one point selling 23 units per second: Corey Gunther, "Apple Announces

iPhone 5 as Fastest Selling Phone in History," *SlashGear*, October 23, 2012, http://www.slashgear.com/apple-announces-iphone-5-as-fastest-selling-phone-in-history-23253373/.

23 *Nintendo began its life*: Nintendo's history is nicely recapped by Tegan Jones, "The Surprisingly Long History of Nintendo," *Gizmodo*, November 20, 2013, http://gizmodo.com/the-surprisingly-long-history-of-nintendo-1354286257 (accessed February 17, 2014).

23 *novelist James Patterson*: Patterson himself declared that he's sold 275 million copies of his books: James Patterson, "Meet James Patterson," jamespatterson.co.uk, http://www.jamespatterson.co.uk/about/ (accessed February 15, 2014).

24 *Award-winning actress*: Zoe Saldana was a ballet dancer, then got her first film role as a ballet dancer in *Center Stage*: "Zoe Saldana," *Biography*, http://www.biography.com/people/zoe-saldana-20906287 (accessed February 15, 2014).

24 *"Startups that pivot"*: Max Marmer, Ertan Dogrultan, Bjoern Lasse Herrmann, and Ron Berman, "Startup Genome Report," *Startup Compass*, no. 1.1 (2011): 5.

26 *If there was ever*: Andrew Johnson's story is captured in brief at "Andrew Johnson," *Biography*, http://www.biography.com/people/andrew-johnson-9355722 (accessed February 15, 2014).

27 *"worked in a groove"*: James Ford Rhodes, *History of the United States from the Compromise of 1850: 1864–1866* (Macmillan, 1904), 589.

27 *"If I can make it there, I'll make it anywhere"*: "Frank Sinatra—New York New York Lyrics," *Rock Genius*, http://rock.rapgenius.com/Frank-sinatra-new-york-new-york-lyrics (accessed February 15, 2014).

28 *Indeed, polls indicate that*: "Is a strong and decisive leader" is twice as important to American voters in both parties (which 77 percent say is "absolutely essential") than "Has a lot of experience in government" (which 34 percent say is "absolutely essential"): "Republicans and Democrats Seek Similar Qualities in 44th President," Gallup, April 4, 2007, http://www.gallup.com/poll/27088/republicans-democrats-seek-similar-qualities-44th-president.aspx.

29 *Why don't we ask the ten*: America's best and worst presidents, ranked by 65 presidential historians based on "public persuasion," "crisis leadership," "economic management," "moral authority," "international relations," "administrative skills," "relations with Congress," "vision/setting an agenda," "pursued equal justice for all," and "performance

within the context of his times": "Historians Survey of Presidential Lead-ership," C-SPAN, 2009, http://legacy.c-span.org/PresidentialSurvey/presidential-leadership-survey.aspx (accessed February 15, 2014). While we're at it, the *New York Times* reports that, according to aging expert S. Jay Olshansky, of the University of Illinois at Chicago, presidents tend to live longer than their peers. So their unconventional lives don't seem to sacrifice health for success. Lawrence K. Altman, "Being President Is Tough but Usually Not Fatal, a Study Concludes," *New York Times*, December 6, 2011, http://www.nytimes.com/2011/12/07/health/american-presidents-outlive-other-men-their-age-study-finds.html (accessed February 15, 2014).

30 *and better at the job*: A lack of political savvy wasn't what allowed great presidents to rise so quickly; it was the fact that they didn't play the same game that other politicians did. Abraham Lincoln had spent his adult life studying the law and politics. The point is that it didn't matter that he hadn't spent time in office; he proved his leadership capabilities regardless, and he had the inherent ability to think laterally, which made him an excellent president.

CHAPTER TWO: TRAINING WITH MASTERS

33 *He stood on a small stage*: Much of Jimmy Fallon's story in this chapter comes from interviews with Randi Siegel, Jimmy's first manager. If you would like to hear more of her firsthand story of Jimmy's early career days, she gives an excellent and detailed account at "Randi Siegel," *Blog-TalkRadio*, http://www.blogtalkradio.com/besteveryou/2012/11/14/randi-siegel (last modified 2012). I spent a lot of time talking to people *around* Jimmy Fallon (producers, friends, former colleagues), and after making it through two layers of NBC publicists, got stuck on Jimmy's personal publicist, who returned one message and then got busy as Jimmy transitioned from *Late Night* to *The Tonight Show*. After two dozen attempts to recontact her by phone, e-mail, and LinkedIn, and at least one attempt to smooth talk my way past security at 30 Rock, I gave up. IF YOU READ THIS, JIMMY, AND WANT TO HANG OUT, DM ME ON TWITTER @SHANESNOW!

33 *the most Emmy-nominated television show*: *Saturday Night Live* has, at the time of this writing, received 171 Emmy nominations: "Awards Search: Saturday Night Live," *Emmys*, http://www.emmys.com/awards/nominations/award-search (accessed February 15, 2014).

33 *the oldest stand-up comedy showcase*: The title of world's longest-running showcase comedy club is self-proclaimed by The Comic Strip: "About the Comic Strip Live Comedy Club," http://www.comicstriplive.com/index.php/about-us/ (accessed February 15, 2014). This claim appears to be undisputed.

36 *spent 15 years performing*: Louis C.K.'s agonizing and amazing journey is documented by Jonah Weiner. "How Louis C.K. Became the Darkest, Funniest Comedian in America," *Rolling Stone*, December 22, 2011, http://www.rollingstone.com/movies/news/how-louis-c-k-became-the-darkest-funniest-comedian-in-america-20111212. C.K. also tops the list at "The 50 Funniest People Now," *Rolling Stone*, http://www.rollingstone.com/culture/lists/the-50-funniest-people-now-20130124/louis-c-k-19691231 (accessed February 15, 2014).

37 *played a few songs on YouTube*: Justin Bieber's story so far is laid out in a simple timeline at "Celebrity Central: Justin Bieber," *People*, http://www.people.com/people/justin_bieber/biography/.

38 *Socrates mentored young Plato*: It is generally known that Plato was Socrates's student and that Aristotle was Plato's. Much of what we know of Socrates actually comes from Plato's writings, as none of Socrates's actual writings appears to have survived. From Plato's writings, we gather that Socrates was his dear friend and mentor, though a few scholars disagree on whether that's the case due to the lack of a direct statement from Plato stating such. The mentorship chain from Socrates to Plato to Aristotle to Alexander is outlined in Philip Freeman, *Alexander the Great* (Simon and Schuster, 2011), 25. And one of the best online sources for quick biographical information on each of these men is compiled by researchers James Fieser and Bradley Dowden, *Internet Encyclopedia of Philosophy* (blog), http://www.iep.utm.edu/ (accessed February 15, 2014).

38 *adventure stories often adhere to a template*: The comprehensive text on the hero's journey is Joseph Campbell, *The Hero with a Thousand Faces* (Princeton University Press, 1972).

38 *Research from Brunel University*: There has been much discussion about the role of practice versus talent since Dr. K. Anders Ericsson of Florida State University showed how "deliberate practice" can produce experts in sports and cognitively complex fields like chess, in spite of (and as a necessary supplement to) natural talent. (Malcolm Gladwell popularized Ericsson's findings as the "10,000 hour rule" in his excellent 2008 book, *Outliers: The Story of Success*.) Further research on chess players, in

particular, has showed that in addition to deliberate practice, training with a great coach increases students' competition performance: Guillermo Campitelli and Fernand Gobet, "The Role of Domain-Specific Practice, Handedness and Starting Age in Chess," *Developmental Psychology* 41, no. 1 (2007): 159–72. Chess prodigy Josh Waitzkin writes about his personal experience on the road to chess championships with mentor Bruce Pandolfini in his memoir, *The Art of Learning* (Free Press, 2007).

39   *Business research backs this up*: Technology industry research by Startup Compass, a group advised by entrepreneurship scholar Steve Blank of Stanford University, shows that mentors have a significant effect on the success of startups: Max Marmer, Ertan Dogrultan, Bjoern Lasse Herrmann, and Ron Berman, "Startup Genome Report Extra on Premature Scaling," *Startup Compass*, no. 1.1 (2011): 8.

39   *Even Steve Jobs*: Football coach Bill Campbell, an eminent ladder switcher who ran Intuit and invested in technology companies for many years, has mentored some of Silicon Valley's most successful entrepreneurs: Jennifer Reingold, "The Secret Coach," *Fortune*, July 21, 2008, http://money.cnn.com/2008/07/21/technology/reingold_coach.fortune/ (accessed February 15, 2014).

39   *equal amounts of research*: Negative mentorship experiences have been documented by various research over the decades. Common reasons attributed to negative outcomes from mentorship include "values," "work style," "personality," "neglect," "credit taking," "personal problems," "inappropriate delegation," and "self-absorption." For a review of the research see Lillian T. Eby, Stacy E. McManus, Shana A. Simon, and Joyce E. A. Russell, "The Protege's Perspective Regarding Negative Mentoring Experiences: The Development of a Taxonomy," *Journal of Vocational Behavior* 57, no. 1 (2000): 1–21.

40   *by family businesses*: The 70 percent statistic about family businesses failing when passed to the second-generation comes via oft-cited research from McKinsey & Co. In a 2010 article, the *Wall Street Journal*'s John Warrillow suggests that the reasons second-generation owners often don't succeed are because (1) they lack the "scratch and claw" drive necessary to manage a business (because they are handed success rather than learning discipline to keep it going) and (2) formal education is not adequate preparation for running a business. The assumption is that business-owner parents often leave the "mentoring" to schools. John Warrillow,

"Leave the Business to the Kids? Maybe Not," *Wall Street Journal*, June 10, 2010, http://online.wsj.com/news/articles/SB1000142405274870457 5304575296523166009344 (accessed February 15, 2014).

41 *"I'd done a transplant"*: Victor E. Sower, Jo Ann Duffy, and Gerald Kohers, "Ferrari's Formula One Handovers and Handovers from Surgery to Intensive Care," *American Society for Quality* (August 2008). The Great Ormond Street handover story is laid out in detail in the above case study and the following journal article: Ken R. Catchpole, Marc R. De Leval, Angus McEwan, Nick Pigott, Martin J. Elliott, Annette McQuillan, Carol Macdonald, and Allan J. Goldman, "Patient Handover from Surgery to Intensive Care: Using Formula 1 Pit-Stop and Aviation Models to Improve Safety and Quality," *Pediatric Anesthesia*, 17 (2007): 470–78.

43 *The answer comes from the research*: Christina M. Underhill, "The Effectiveness of Mentoring Programs in Corporate Settings: A Meta-analytical Review of the Literature," *Journal of Vocational Behavior* 68 (2006): 292–307, shows that informal mentoring has a greater effect than formal mentoring. A later study found that formal and informal mentorship results in various activities (work, youth, academic) were small, but generally positive: Lillian T. Eby, Tammy D. Allen, Sarah C. Evans, Thomas Ng, and David L. DuBois, "Does Mentoring Matter? A Multidisciplinary Meta-Analysis Comparing Mentored and Non-mentored Individuals," *Journal of Vocational Behavior* 72, no. 2 (2008): 254–67.

44 *"Searching for a mentor has become the professional equivalent"*: Sheryl Sandberg, *Lean In: Women, Work, and the Will to Lead* (Alfred A. Knopf, 2013).

46 *journey-focused mentorship and not just a focus on practice*: Further research shows that when protégés open up to their mentors—what my friend and NextJump.com founder Charlie Kim calls "vulnerability"—they tend to achieve more positive results: Connie R. Wanberg, Elizabeth T. Welsh, and John Kammeyer-Mueller, "Protege and Mentor Self-Disclosure: Levels and Outcomes within Formal Mentoring Dyads in a Corporate Context," *Journal of Vocational Behavior* 70, no. 2 (2007): 398–412.

46 *"We were kids without fathers"*: Jay-Z, *Decoded* (Spiegel and Grau, 2010).

47 *"Most everything I've done, I've copied"*: Sam Walton and John Huey, *Sam Walton: Made in America* (Bantam, 1993).

47 *"first-class noticer"*: This phrase comes from Saul Bellow, *The Actual: A*

Novella (Penguin Classics, 2009). Noticing tiny details makes the difference between faster and slower learners. "Because of their ability to see patterns of meaningful information, experts begin problem solving at 'a higher place,'" according to National Research Council, *How People Learn* (National Academies Press, 2000), 33–48.

49 *found himself once again on stage*: You can view Jimmy Fallon's second *SNL* audition at "Jimmy Fallon's SNL Audition," YouTube, http://www .youtube.com/watch?v=u1aKiolG2CA (accessed February 15, 2014).

50 *The world's youngest Nobel Prize winner*: Lawrence Bragg won the Nobel Prize for physics in 1915 with his father, William, for birthing a new scientific field: X-ray crystallography. More of Lawrence's story can be read at "The Parent Trap," NobelPrize.org, http://www.nobelprize. org/nobel_prizes/physics/laureates/1915/perspectives.html   (accessed February 15, 2014).

50 *The billion-dollar micro-blogging service*: This January 2013 *Forbes* cover story delivers a great history of David Karp's journey: Jeff Bercovici, "Tumblr: David Karp's $800 Million Art Project," *Forbes*, January 2013.

51 *"He was a beacon for me"*: "Louis C.K. Honors George Carlin," New York Public Library, http://www.youtube.com/watch?v=R37zkizucPU (accessed February 15, 2014).

CHAPTER THREE: RAPID FEEDBACK

53 *The most popular post*: Though the *Upworthy* blog and its content was overseen by Pariser, the seven blunders story was "posted" by his editorial director: Sara Critchfield, "The 7 Warnings from Gandhi in the Final Hours of His Life," *Upworthy*, http://www.upworthy.com/the-7-warnings-from-gandhi-in-the-final-hours-of-his-life (accessed May 27, 2013). At the time I checked the Facebook statistics, the story had received 12 shares; however that count may increase as more people discover it.

53 *the top story on the hugely popular blog*: The *BuzzFeed* article about '90s side characters is by Dave Stopera, "20 Supporting Characters from '90s TV Shows Then and Now," *BuzzFeed*, March 27, 2012, http:// www.buzzfeed.com/daves4/20-supporting-actors-from-90s-tv-shows-then-and-n (accessed May 27, 2013). I actually did laugh at the Olmec reference.

54 *a mellow, unshaven author*: Eli Pariser is author of a fascinating book

about one of the darker effects of the "personalized" Internet, *The Filter Bubble: What the Internet Is Hiding from You* (Penguin Press, 2011).

54 *including Facebook cofounder*: Upworthy's investor information can be found at CrunchBase, *Upworthy*, http://www.crunchbase.com/company/ upworthy (accessed February 15, 2014).

55 *the week after* Upworthy *launched*: The baby meerkats and other disappointed animals can be found at Jack Shepherd, "33 Animals Who Are Extremely Disappointed in You," *BuzzFeed*, April 10, 2012, http://www .buzzfeed.com/expresident/animals-who-are-extremely-disappointed-in-you (accessed May 27, 2013).

56 *The little comedy theater*: You can learn everything you want about Kelly Leonard, executive director of The Second City, and the school itself at The Second City, https://www.secondcity.com. NPR lists various stars to emerge from the school, and quotes the thing about "Harvard of ha-ha" from author Mike Thomas at David Schaper, "The Second City at 50: The Harvard of Ha Ha," NPR, December 11, 2009, http://www.npr.org/ templates/story/story.php?storyId=121355679 (accessed February 15, 2014). See also: Mike Thomas, *The Second City Unscripted: Revolution and Revelation at the World-Famous Comedy Theater* (Villard, 2009).

59 *"Fail often" is a guiding aphorism*: "Fail fast, fail often" is a much-chanted mantra of Silicon Valley as of the mid-2000s, and is attributed variously to gurus like Seth Godin and Eric Ries. The earliest published attribution I could find is a 1997 quote attributed to IDEO founder David Kelley: Anna Muoio, "They Have a Better Idea . . . Do You?" *Fast Company*, August 31, 1997. http://www.fastcompany.com/29116/ they-have-better-idea-do-you.

59 *"Here you only get one chance"*: Mure Dickie, "Stigma of Failure Holds Back Japan Start-Ups," *Financial Times*, February 22, 2011. http://www .ft.com/cms/s/0/abb1facc-3eb0-11e0-834e-00144feabdc0.html (accessed February 15, 2014). The dishonor surrounding business failure in countries like Japan in years past is troubling, though the trend seems to be reversing with the advent of more high-tech startups adopting the Silicon Valley style. However, while being allowed to try again after failing is important, research from both Harvard and Startup Compass show that merely failing does not equal learning, nor does it mean much better chances for next time. According to Harvard research conducted in 2008 and published in 2010, entrepreneurs who took companies public are 30 percent more likely to do it again, while founders who've failed are 22

percent more likely to take a new company public, and brand-new entrepreneurs are 21 percent more likely to do so: Paul Gompers, Anna Kovner, Josh Lerner, and David Scharfstein, "Performance Persistence in Entrepreneurship," *Journal of Financial Economics* 96 (2010): 18–32. That's a 50 percent greater chance of success for the already-successful entrepreneur, and negligible increase in likelihood for the failed entrepreneur over a newbie. The Startup Genome Report from chapter 1 demonstrates that these findings are also true among technology companies that succeed at a smaller scale than IPO: Max Marmer, Ertan Dogrultan, Bjoern Lasse Herrmann, and Ron Berman, "Startup Genome Report," *Startup Compass,* no 1.1 (2011): 1–67.

61   *NBA star Michael Jordan*: In a 1998 Nike advertisement, Michael Jordan said, "I've missed more than 9,000 shots in my career. I've lost almost 300 games. Twenty-six times I've been trusted to take the game-winning shot and missed. I've failed over and over again in my life. And that is why I succeed." Robert Goldman and Stephen Papson, *Nike Culture: The Sign of the Swoosh* (Sage, 1998), 49.

61   *one-third of hospital patient volume*: The CABG study, risks of neurological complications, and Staats's "paradox of failure" are presented in a well-documented paper: Bradley R. Staats, KC Diwas, and Francesca Gino, "Learning from My Success and from Others' Failure: Evidence from Minimally Invasive Cardiac Surgery," *Management Science* 59, no. 11 (2013): 2435–49.

68   *a hundred years of these studies*: Kluger and DeNisi examine the "contradictory and seldom straight-forward" outcomes of feedback intervention studies over the decades in Avraham N. Kluger and Angelo DeNisi, "The Effects of Feedback Interventions on Performance: A Historical Review, a Meta-Analysis, and a Preliminary Feedback Intervention Theory," *Psychological Bulletin* 119, no. 2 (1996): 254–84, and find that more than one-third of feedback decreases performance. "The results suggest that FI [feedback intervention] effectiveness decreases as attention moves up the hierarchy closer to the self and away from the task," they write.

68   *vastly preferred negative feedback*: As people gain expertise, they shift from desiring positive feedback to desiring negative, write Stacey R. Finkelstein and Ayelet Fishbach, "Tell Me What I Did Wrong: Experts Seek and Respond to Negative Feedback," *Journal of Consumer Research Inc.,* no. 39 (2011): 22–38. "Positive feedback increased

novices' commitment, and negative feedback increased experts' sense that they were making insufficient progress," they find. This dovetails with The Second City's method for training its students: year one is about making students comfortable and confident; year two is about showing them what they're doing wrong and getting them to take bigger leaps.

69   *This gets at the principle of rapid*: Research shows that the speed of the feedback loop is important: managers who get occasional feedback on their work tend to improve more slowly than those who get repeated feedback, according to Charles F. Seifert and Gary Yukl, "Effects of Repeated Multi-Source Feedback on the Influence Behavior and Effectiveness of Managers: A Field Experiment," *Leadership Quarterly* 21 (2010): 856–66.

A few salient quotes from this article are enlightening:

> People react in different ways to negative feedback, and little change is likely to occur unless a person is willing to acknowledge deficiencies indicated by the feedback. (857)
> Negative feedback is more likely to be accepted and applied by someone with strong self confidence and emotional maturity. (857)
> Even when feedback recipients have good intentions about improving their behavior, little actual improvement is likely unless they remain focused on implementing their plans for using the feedback. (857)

In an interesting counterweight to Weick's "small wins," Sim B. Sitkin, "Learning through Failure: The Strategy of Small Losses," *Research in Organizational Behavior* 14 (1992): 231–66, proposes that designing for "small losses" can prevent systemic failure. Sitkin calls this strategy "intelligent failure," and writes, "Failure should not be pursued for its own sake. It is a means to an end, not the end itself. If the goal is learning, then unanticipated failure is the unavoidable byproduct associated with the risks inherent in addressing challenging problems." Additional study indicates that, in Sitkin's words, "The faster the action-failure-action cycle, the more feedback that can be gathered and used for adjustments . . . learning is facilitated when information is quickly generated, evaluated, and adjusted to."

71 *Not long ago, on a sleepy*: The Zach Sobiech video can be found at "My Last Days: Meet Zach Sobiech," Soul Pancake, http://www.youtube.com/watch?v=9NjKgV65fpo (accessed February 15, 2014).

72 *the fastest-growing media company*: *Business Insider* did the math and declared *Upworthy* the fastest-growing media company in history here: Alyson Shontell, "How to Create the Fastest Growing Media Company in the World," *Business Insider*, November 5, 2012. http://www.business insider.com/upworthy-how-to-create-a-fast-growing-media-company-2012-11 (accessed February 15, 2014).

73 *a few of the contenders*: The data of the Zach Sobiech headlines is from a private case study called "Advanced Chess," which the *Upworthy* team was kind enough to share with me.

CHAPTER FOUR: PLATFORMS

81 *That's what computer programming is like*: Abstraction in computer science is certainly more complex in practice than one can convey in a few paragraphs like I have in this chapter. For detailed reading on the subject, I suggest Timothy R. Colburn, *Philosophy and Computer Science* (M. E. Sharpe, 1999), chapter 11. If you're really hungry, the books in this list will keep you going for a while: "A Reading List for the Self-Taught Computer Scientist," *Reddit*, http://www.reddit.com/r/books/comments/ch0wt/a_reading_list_for_the_selftaught_computer/ (accessed February 16, 2014).

85 *He called it Ruby on Rails*: For more information on Ruby on Rails, see http://rubyonrails.org/.

85 *a couple of guys at a podcasting startup*: For a thorough and dramatic history of Twitter, see Nick Bilton, *Hatching Twitter: A True Story of Money, Power, Friendship, and Betrayal* (Portfolio, 2013).

86 *"standing on the shoulders of giants"*: The common contemporary quotation comes from a line in one of Sir Isaac Newton's letters to Robert Hooke: "If I have seen further, it is by standing on ye shoulders of Giants," Newton, letter to Hooke, February 5, 1676, http://www.isa acnewton.org.uk/essays/Giants. The phrase appears to have originated with Bernard of Chartres in the 12th century: Robert K. Merton, *On the Shoulders of Giants* (Free Press, 1965).

86 *managed to be the best with less effort*: Robert Compton directed Dr. Tony Wagner's documentary in which the fascinating statistics about Finland's education system are brought forth and explained: Robert

Compton, *The Finland Phenomenon* (2011), IMDb, http://www.imdb
.com/title/tt2101464/. Wagner's books are further helpful in under-
standing the environments in which innovative students can be trained:
Tony Wagner, *Creating Innovators: The Making of Young People Who
Will Change the World* (Scribner, 2012), and *The Global Achievement
Gap: Why Even Our Best Schools Don't Teach the New Survival Skills
Our Children Need—and What We Can Do about It* (Basic Books,
2008).

87 *teachers in Finland spent about half*: Jim Hull, "Time in School: How
Does the U.S. Compare?," Center for Public Education, December 2011,
http://www.centerforpubliceducation.org/Main-Menu/Organizing-a-
school/Time-in-school-How-does-the-US-compare (accessed February
16, 2014).

87 *"I think it's a great mistake"*: My interview with Freeman Dyson was
one of the more fascinating I conducted for this book. Dyson spoke pas-
sionately about hands-on learning being a catalyst for skill and interest
development, and about how traditional sit-and-think-about-it education was counterproductive for young people. "I learned much more
in museums than I did in school," he said. "But having people drilled,
that just turns them off." In our discussion of tools for calculation, he
said that a danger of digital tools occurs when they make mathematics
more complex, such as when a calculator counts to nine figures of accuracy. However, he believes computation aids, especially if they can
be put into some sort of physical world context, are enormously helpful
to understanding underlying concepts. The slide rule in particular, he
said, was an excellent platform for that reason. "It's a good way of getting the feeling of magnitude. You feel it in your hands," he said. "It's
a shame, because it's really easy to understand. It's accurate enough for
almost all purposes."

89 *or learning by making and manipulating objects*: Seymour Papert and
Idit Harel's tome on constructionism is rare to find in print, but the
first chapter is accessible online at Papert and Harel, *Situating Constructionism* (Ablex, 1991), http://www.papert.org/articles/Situating
Constructionism.html. Papert's book on kids and computers is a must-
read when exploring the topic of platform-enhanced learning: Papert,
Mindstorms: Children, Computers, and Powerful Ideas (Basic Books,
1993).

90 *students who use calculators have better attitudes*: Results from 54

research studies on calculators in precollege education showed that "students' operational skills and problem-solving skills improved when calculators were an integral part of testing and instruction" and that "calculator use did not hinder the development of mathematical skills. Students using calculators had better attitudes toward mathematics than their noncalculator counterparts." Aimee J. Ellington, "A Meta-Analysis of the Effects of Calculators on Students' Achievement and Attitude Levels in Precollege Mathematics Classes," *Journal for Research in Mathematics Education* 34, no. 5 (2003): 433–63. The attitude factor is crucial to the development of young people who may eventually become innovators in STEM, which is why *Hopscotch* (https://www.gethopscotch.com/), *Mindstorms* (http://www.lego.com/en-us/mindstorms/?domainredir= mindstorms.lego.com), and other *building*-based educational games are so important. In particular, I recommend mastering statistics in high school through games like *Blackjack* and *Yahtzee*, and the teaching of personal finance through money arbitrage and debt simulations like the classic DOS game *Drugwars* (although somebody really ought to invent a PG version of this for kids).

91   *coauthored more than sixty books*: Dave Moursund was quite helpful to me as I thought through this chapter and he helped to tether the calculator discussion to the priority of high-order thinking in mathematics. Browse a comprehensive archive of his articles online at Moursund, "Dr. Dave Moursund's Writing about Computers in Education," University of Oregon, November 11, 2007, http://pages.uoregon.edu/moursund/dave/ (accessed February 16, 2014).

91   *"Mathematics is a way of thinking"* and *"Get the thinking right"*: Keith Devlin, "In Math You Have to Remember, in Other Subjects You Can Think about It," *Mathematical Association of America*, June 2010, http://www.maa.org/external_archive/devlin/devlin_06_10.html (accessed February 16, 2014). This essay and Devlin's book, *The Math Gene: How Mathematical Thinking Evolved and Why Numbers Are Like Gossip* (Basic Books, 2001), are must-reads on what's wrong with mathematics education today in light of the tools we have at our disposal and the way we think about other subjects. Studies show that humans have the innate ability to grasp math, but that focusing on calculation skills is much less productive than focusing on thinking and real-world challenges. Profoundly, such calculation skills come naturally through such methods. Devlin closes his essay by pointing out exactly the

challenge that Finland managed to solve with its teachers: "Of course, teaching math in the progressive way requires teachers with more mathematical knowledge than does the traditional approach (where a teacher with a weaker background can simply follow the textbook—which incidentally is why American math textbooks are so thick). It is also much more demanding to teach that way, which makes it a job that deserves a far higher status and better pay-scale than are presently the case." And one final barb at memorization from Tony Wagner: "We all had to learn the periodic table in high school. Well how many of us can recite the periodic table today? Or even tell you how many elements there are and if you came up with a number you'd be wrong because two more were added last month."

92 *problem solving is more valuable*: Dudley Underwood, "Is Mathematics Necessary?," National Council of Teachers of Mathematics, 1998, http://www.public.iastate.edu/~aleand/dudley.html (accessed February 16, 2014).

93 *building a road out of mud*: I should note that I believe that most teachers want nothing more than for their kids to succeed, regardless of their qualifications. Keith Devlin puts it well: "What you find are thousands of teachers doing the best they can, trying to balance the need for conceptual understanding with the need to practice basic skills, but unsure of what is the best way to proceed, particularly when it comes to motivating their students. In the meantime, absent any clear evidence as to how best proceed, the majority of teachers quite understandably default to more or less the same teaching methods that they themselves experienced. Overwhelmingly that is the traditional method, though the fact that no one has been able to make this approach work (for the majority of students) in three-thousand years does make some wonder if there is a better way."

93 *"The definition of insanity"*: Though variously attributed to Albert Einstein and Mark Twain, this phrase seems to have first appeared in *World Service Conference* (Narcotics Anonymous, 1981), 11.

95 *Finnish schools allowed students unrestricted use of calculators*: *Science and Engineering Indicators 2002* (National Science Board, 2002), chapter 1. Though Tony Wagner's research and international test scores indicate that Finland's education trump all in a 2009 journal article in the *Teaching of Mathematics*, Olli Martio demonstrates that many Finnish students (the bottom 80 percent) had poorer high-level mental

math skills in 2003 than in 1981, and blames the use of calculators and the omission of geometry curricula. Martio makes the same mistake as many critics in taking for granted that mental algebraic skills are a necessary baseline for success in life, but does correctly indicate that much of the math curriculum in Finland and other countries exists in its present form because at some point "somebody has thought them useful," and that periodic reevaluation is necessary. Though Martio's conclusions from Finnish math test results beg basic questions, he points out that the top 20 percent of students indeed enter the work force well prepared for careers. Olli Martio, "Long Term Effects in Learning Mathematics in Finland—Curriculum Changes and Calculators," *Teaching of Mathematics* 12, no. 2 (2009): 51–56. A proliferation of research shows that calculators positively affect students' ability to do mathematics. This depends, as the other research in this chapter would lead us to expect, on how the thinking behind calculator use is taught. Edward W. Wolfe of Pearson Assessments writes that it is "clear from the most recent studies that [judicious] use of the calculator, use of the right type of calculator, and integration of the calculator into mathematics instruction are keys to maximizing the positive impact" on tests. His essay, and a host of reference studies, can be found at Wolfe, "What Impact Does Calculator Use Have on Test Results?" *Pearson Education Test, Measurement & Research Services Bulletin,* no. 14 (2010), http://images. pearsonassessments.com/images/tmrs/tmrs_rg/Bulletin_14.pdf?WT .mc_id=TMRS_What_Impact_Does_Calculator.

95   *Finland created a higher educational platform*: The definitive book on Finland's education system is by Pasi Sahlberg, *Finnish Lessons: What Can the World Learn from Educational Change in Finland?* (Teachers College Press, 2011).

95   *international rankings dropped a few slots*: In 2013, when Finland's international PISA (Programme for International Student Assessment) test rankings slipped in some categories, Pasi Sahlberg noted the following in the *Wall Street Journal*:

> The unexpected position as a global educational leader and role model may have disturbed Finland's previous commitment to continuous improvement and renewal. Some argue that complacency and focus on explaining the past to thousands of education tourists have shifted attention away from developing Finland's

own school system. Others contend that the high-profile of PISA have led other nations to alter their curricula. Such observers point to the usage of PISA questions to shape lessons and coaching students to take PISA-like tests. As a norm-referenced test, PISA is graded on a curve. What other nations have learned from Finland and put into practice has necessarily brought down Finland's results.

Sahlberg, "Are Finland's Vaunted Schools Slipping?" *Washington Post*, December 3, 2013, http://www.washingtonpost.com/blogs/answer-sheet/wp/2013/12/03/are-finlands-vaunted-schools-slipping/ (accessed February 15, 2014).

A final noteworthy fact that often goes unnoticed in the Finnish education discussion is that there are no private schools in Finland. Sahlberg writes, "The Finnish school system continues to be one of the most equitable among the OECD countries. This means that in Finland, students' learning in school is less affected by their family backgrounds than in most other countries."

95 *coined the term "lateral thinking" in 1967*: Edward de Bono expounds on this and other terminology on his official website: "Lateral Thinking," http://edwdebono.com/lateral.htm (accessed February 16, 2014).

98 *Is it any wonder*: Big cities are epicenters for invention, according to patent filings as collected and reported by Jonathan Rothwell, José Lobo, Deborah Strumsky, and Mark Muro, "Patenting Prosperity: Invention and Economic Performance in the United States and Its Metropolitan Areas," Brookings, 2013, http://www.brookings.edu/~/media/research/files/reports/2013/02/patenting prosperity rothwell/patenting prosperity rothwell.pdf (accessed February 15, 2014). The authors write that "Sixty-three percent of U.S. patents are developed by people living in just 20 metro areas, which are home to 34 percent of the U.S. population." Richard Florida writes about the benefits of city living for creative people in *The Rise of the Creative Class—Revisited: 10th Anniversary Edition—Revised and Expanded*, 2nd edition (Basic Books, 2012) and argues that creative people may actually boost the economics of cities, though many have debated whether this is causation or correlation. Jonah Lehrer writes about "urban friction" as a key reason for creativity and invention in big cities in *Imagine: How Creativity Works* (Houghton Mifflin, 2012). (*Imagine* was pulled from shelves due

to factual issues in other chapters, but the "urban friction" section itself checked out, scandal free.)

CHAPTER FIVE: WAVES

102 *Quick etymology lesson*: A thorough definition of screamo can be found, of course, at "Screamo," *Urban Dictionary*, http://www.urbandictio nary.com/define.php?term=screamo (accessed February 16, 2014).

106 *A wave is made up of*: An excellent (and visual) primer on ocean wave science comes from Richard Mitterer, "Ocean Waves," University of Texas at Dallas, http://www.utdallas.edu/~mitterer/Oceanography/pdfs/ OCEChapt09.pdf (accessed February 16, 2014).

108 *clips from some basketball games for extra credit*: The basketball and handbag intuition-versus-pattern-recognition studies come from Erik Dane, Kevin W. Rockmann, and Michael G. Pratt, "When Should I Trust My Gut? Linking Domain Expertise to Intuitive Decision-Making Effectiveness," *Organizational Behavior and Human Decision Processes* 119 (2012): 187–194. My interview with Dane yielded many more fascinating insights on the subject, which could not fit in the book. I've published much of that supplementary material at shanesnow.com/dane.

111 *constantly tinkering with potential trends*: Ryan Tate's book on "20% time" outlines the research and stories about business experimentation à la 3M and Google better than any collection of research I could put here. I encourage you to check it out: Tate, *The 20% Doctrine: How Tinkering, Goofing Off, and Breaking the Rules at Work Drive Success in Business* (HarperBusiness, 2012). For an excellent academic discussion about experimentation for entrenched businesses, see Stefan Thomke, "Unlocking Innovation through Business Experimentation," *European Business Review*, http://www.europeanbusinessreview.com/?p=8420 (accessed February 17, 2014).

112 *enjoy an unfair advantage over their competitors*: The seminal paper on first-mover advantage was Marvin B. Lieberman, and David B. Montgomery, "First-Mover Advantages," *Strategic Management Journal*, no. 9 (1988): 41–58. Lieberman and Montgomery revisited and amended their claims ten years later in "First-Mover (Dis)Advantages: Retrospective and Link with the Resource-Based View," *Strategic Management Journal* 19 (1998): 1111–25. I pick on Ken Lerer a little bit in this section and I confess that I think he understands the complexities of the subject better than he let on in that class full of beginners. And I must disclose

that his venture capital fund once declined to make an investment in my company (which his business partner later said he regretted having done, live on Bloomberg TV), so there is a tiny chance that I relished the opportunity to deliver a friendly jab here.

115 *47 percent of first movers* failed: Peter N. Golder and Gerard J. Tellis, "Pioneer Advantage: Marketing Logic or Marketing Legend?" *Journal of Marketing Research* 30 (1993): 158–70. Other articles that proved crucial to this chapter's discussion include Robert A. Baron, "Opportunity Recognition as Pattern Recognition: How Entrepreneurs 'Connect the Dots' to Identify," *Academy of Management Perspectives* 20, no. 1 (2006): 104–119, http://old.ied.econ.msu.ru/cmt2/lib/c/186/File/fa4_1.pdf (accessed February 16, 2014), and Daniel Kahneman and Gary Klein, "Conditions for Intuitive Expertise," *American Psychologist* 64, no. 6 (September 2009): 515–26, as well as William P. Barnett, Mi Feng, and Xaioqu Luo, "Social Identity, Market Memory, and First-Mover Advantage," *Industrial and Corporate Change* 22, no. 3 (2012): 585.

116 *Fast followers, on the other hand*: Reasons for the second-wave advantage were proposed by researchers from Texas A&M only a few years after Lieberman and Montgomery's initial paper on first movers. "Major shifts in technology for which the first mover is ill-prepared because of its investment in old technology may favor the fast follower that is not burdened with such investments," write Roger A. Kerin, P. Rajan Varadarajan, and Robert A. Peterson, "First-Mover Advantage: A Synthesis, Conceptual Framework, and Research Propositions," *Journal of Marketing* 56, no. 4 (1992): 33–52. "Later entrants' access to relatively newer cost-efficient technologies enables them to offset or neutralize the first mover's experience-based cost advantages."

116 *Many of the biggest corporate successes*: Steve Blank, writing in *Business Insider*, makes one of the best-formed arguments on second-wave advantage out there: "You're Better Off Being a Fast Follower than an Originator," *Business Insider*, October 5, 2010, http://www.businessinsider.com/youre-better-off-being-a-fast-follower-than-an-originator-2010-10 (accessed February 16, 2014).

117 *The way to predict the best waves*: Fernando F. Suarez and Gianvito Lanzolla, "The Role of Environmental Dynamics in Building a First Mover Advantage Theory," *Academy of Management Review* 32, no. 2 (2007): 377–92

120 *In the past three years, Skrillex*: At the time of this writing, Sonny Moore

had won Grammys for best dance recording (twice), best dance/electronica album (twice), and best remixed recording, non-classical (twice). Sonny was kind and generous with his time (as was his publicist Clayton Blaha). The kid explodes with feeling; at times, I felt like I was talking to Andy Warhol. Example quote: "It's not fine art composition, ya know—it's not something to f—ing pick apart; it's something you feel immediately. And, like, that's how my life's just been; it's so fast-paced, about feeling, it's about making it happen, ya know, and the experiencing it as well. To constantly take things in and respond to that. I love to push it out and see what I feel, like I have something in me." Sonny works hard at his music—I've seen him practicing furiously two minutes before he was supposed to be on stage, getting new material down in order to give his fans something special—and I'm convinced that he's been able to catch his waves because he's *constantly* experimenting. But he also has a knack for *feeling* when the water rises. He's the kind of guy who could probably surf blindfolded.

> *There is a tide in the affairs of men*
> *Which, taken at the flood, leads on to fortune;*
> *Omitted, all the voyage of their life*
> *Is bound in shallows and in miseries.*

William Shakespeare, *Julius Caesar*, http://www.shakespeare-online.com/plays/julius_4_3.html. (Hat tip to Robert Baron.)

CHAPTER SIX: SUPERCONNECTORS

123 *Playa Las Coloradas, on the southern*: Descriptions of Cuba, its geography, and the *manglar rojo* came from Nicki Agate, *The Rough Guide to the Caribbean: More than 50 Islands, Including the Bahamas* (Rough Guides, 2002), http://books.google.com/books?id=gWoW8qZogSQC (accessed February 15, 2014), 203; "Square Miles in Cuba," *Wolfram Alpha*, http://www.wolframalpha.com/input/?i=square miles in cuba (accessed February 15, 2014); "Sierra Maestra," *Encyclopaedia Britannica*, http://www.britannica.com/EBchecked/topic/356293/Sierra-Maestra (accessed February 15, 2014); "Eastern Cuba Sights," *Fodor's Travel*, http://www.fodors.com/world/caribbean/cuba/eastern-cuba/review-473363.html (accessed February 15, 2014); and T. Ombrello, "Red Mangrove," Union County College, http://faculty.ucc

.edu/biology-ombrello/pow/red_mangrove.htm (accessed February 15, 2014).

124 *Cuba was no stranger to revolution*: The history of the Cuban revolution and Radio Rebelde was compiled from the following tornado of books and sources: Aviva Chomsky, *A History of the Cuban Revolution* (Wiley-Blackwell, 2010); Nancy Stout and Alice Walker, *One Day in December*: *Celia Sanchez and the Cuban Revolution* (Monthly Review Press, 2013); Thomas G. Paterson, *Contesting Castro: The United States and the Triumph of the Cuban Revolution* (Oxford University Press, 1995); John Lee Anderson, *Che Guevara: A Revolutionary Life* (Grove Press, 1997), 299; René de La Pedraja, *Wars of Latin America, 1948–1982: The Rise of the Guerrillas* (McFarland, 2013), 53; Richard L. Harris, *Che Guevara: A Biography* (Greenwood, 2010), 68; Paul J. Dosal, *Comandante Che: Guerrilla Soldier, Commander, and Strategist, 1956–1967* (Penn State University Press, 2004), 177; Paco Ignacio Taibo, *Guevara, Also Known as Che* (Macmillan, 1999), 73; "BBC History—Fidel Castro," BBC, http://www.bbc.co.uk/history/people/fidel_castro (accessed February 15, 2014); Lisa Reynolds Wolfe, "Habaneros Turn on Batista," *Cold War Studies*, http://www.coldwarstudies.com/2013/06/11/habaneros-turn-on-batista/ (accessed February 15, 2014).

125 *"Condemn me. It does not matter"*: Spencer C. Tucker, *Encyclopedia of Insurgency and Counterinsurgency: A New Era of Modern Warfare* (ABC-CLIO, 2013), 126.

129 "Aqui Radio Rebelde!": Hugh Thomas, *Cuba: La lucha por la libertad 1762–1970* (Grijalbo, 1973), 1261.

129 *"made concrete to the whole nation"*: This quotation comes from Ricardo Martinez Victores, *La historia de Radio Rebelde* (Editorial de Ciencias Sociales, 1978), as translated and contextualized by Cat Wiener, "Winning Hearts and Minds: The Importance of Radio in the Cuban Revolutionary War" (2010), http://www.scribd.com/doc/41464197/Radio-Rebelde (accessed February 17, 2014). Wiener's essay contains references to a number of excellent additional sources on Radio Rebelde and pirate radio in revolutionary history.

129 *"The fact that we were outnumbered"*: T. J. English, *Havana Nocturne: How the Mob Owned Cuba and Then Lost It to the Revolution* (William Morrow, 2008).

132 *"I think each one was worse"*: Steven Priggé, "How Famous Writers and Producers Got Their Breaks: J. J. Abrams," *New Show Studios*, January

8, 2013, http://www.newshowstudios.com/blog/television/how-famous-writers-and-producers-got-their-breaks-j-j-abrams/ (accessed February 15, 2014).

132 *When we look at Abrams's subsequent*: You can see Abrams's full filmography at "J. J. Abrams," IMDb, http://www.imdb.com/name/nm0009190/ (accessed February 17, 2014).

133 *"Being a giver doesn't require"*: Adam Grant, *Give and Take: A Revolutionary Approach to Success* (Viking Adult, 2013).

135 *to start a company called Mint*: An excellent recap of the business strategy, content strategy, and superconnecting that went on at Mint Software, Inc. can be found at Zach Bulygo, "How Mint Grew to 1.5 Million Users and Sold for $170 Million in Just 2 Years," *KISSmetrics*, 2013, http://blog.kissmetrics.com/how-mint-grew/ (accessed February 17, 2014). Mint built up demand for its service for months through its blog content *before* it even launched the Mint app to the public. This strategy of manufacturing potential energy before launch is further explored in chapter 7.

137 *"Radio Rebelde truly became"*: Radio Rebelde exists today as a popular radio station in Cuba. This quote is preserved on the station's website: "About Us—Radio Rebelde," Radio Rebelde, http://www.radiorebelde.cu/english/about-us/ (accessed February 15, 2014).

137 *"The radio should be ruled"*: Ernesto Guevara, *Guerrilla Warfare* (BN Publishing, 2013).

138 *Cuba's literacy rate is 99.8 percent*: Reported by the CIA in *The World Factbook* (Central Intelligence Agency, 2011), https://www.cia.gov/library/publications/the-world-factbook/fields/2103.html.

138 *less popular than cockroaches*: The poll about what Americans like better than Congress was conducted via phone interviews of 830 voters during the 112th Congress. While the results are both hilarious and disheartening, the fact that Genghis Khan managed to beat Congress while Congress beat the Kardashians seems to indicate that some Americans do not know what these things are. Congress did rank higher than meth labs and lobbyists, however, which I think we can count as a win in the war against mind-altering substances: "Congress Less Popular than Cockroaches, Traffic Jams," *Public Policy Polling*, January 8, 2013, http://www.publicpolicypolling.com/pdf/2011/PPP_Release_Natl_010813_.pdf (accessed February 15, 2014).

CHAPTER SEVEN: MOMENTUM

141 *"the funniest video in the world"*: Jimmy Kimmel tweeted Bear Vasquez's "Double Rainbow" video with this description. Technically, he quoted his friend, Todd, and agreed that "he might very well be right." Jimmy Kimmel, Twitter tweet, July 3, 2010, https://twitter.com/jimmykimmel/status/17665533038 (accessed February 17, 2014).

142 *"What does it mean"*: Paul Vasquez, "Yosemitebear Mountain Double Rainbow 1-8-10," YouTube, January 8, 2010, http://www.youtube.com/watch?v=OQSNhk5ICTI (accessed February 17, 2014).

143 *second-most-watched female YouTuber*: Phan's channel is "Michelle Phan," YouTube, http://www.youtube.com/user/MichellePhan.

143 *more than 150,000 paying subscribers*: Lauren Sherman, "How Bloggers Are Scoring Million-Dollar Funding Rounds," *Advertising Age*, May 29, 2013, http://adage.com/article/digital/bloggers-capture-venture-capitalist-interest/241687/ (accessed February 17, 2014). The rest of the material for Phan's story comes directly from Phan herself.

143 *"Your entire philosophy of money"*: Robert Frank, *Richistan: A Journey through the American Wealth Boom and the Lives of the New Rich* (Three Rivers Press, 2008).

144 *"pajama rich"*: the phrase "pajama rich" comes from Bill Simmons, "One Night at Jack's Place," *ESPN*, May 5, 2010, http://sports.espn.go.com/espn/page2/story?page=simmons/100505 (accessed February 17, 2014).

144 *"When money is available in near-limitless"*: Manfred Kets de Vries as quoted by Helen Kirwan-Taylor, "Miserable? Bored? You Must Be Rich," *The Telegraph*, November 13, 2007, http://www.telegraph.co.uk/news/features/3634620/Miserable-Bored-You-must-be-rich.html (accessed February 17, 2014).

145 *When businesspeople cash out big*: Sudden-wealth therapists Susan Bradley, Stephen Goldbart, and Joan DiFuria were each quite helpful with the material for the "depressed billionaires" portion of this chapter, both on record and on background. Their books on the subject are: Stephen Goldbart and Joan Indursky DiFuria, *Affluence Intelligence: Earn More, Worry Less, and Live a Happy and Balanced Life* (Da Capo Lifelong Books, 2011) and Susan Bradley, *Sudden Money: Managing a Financial Windfall* (Wiley, 2000). "In our society, money is over-valued as a source of meaning and a symbol of success. That money changes how you see yourself, how you interact with people and what you do with your day and your future in very significant ways," says Goldbart.

145 *If you want to get really depressed*: An excellent CNN story recapping the various journeys of former moonwalkers: Chris Chandler and Andy Rose, "After Walking on Moon, Astronauts Trod Various Paths," CNN, July 17, 2009, http://edition.cnn.com/2009/TECH/07/17/life.after. moon.landing/index.html (accessed February 17, 2014). Original reporting of Armstrong's lawsuits can be seen at Bill Romano, "Neil Armstrong Sues over Use of Name in Ad," *Boca Raton News*, February 6, 1997, http://news.google.com/newspapers?nid=1291&dat=19970206&id= 1ClUAAAAIBAJ&sjid=TY4DAAAAIBAJ&pg=4495,1731221 (accessed February 17, 2014). James Irwin's ministry info can be found in his obituary at "James Irwin Was Astronaut, Minister, City Native," Associated Press, August 10, 1991, http://news.google.com/news papers?nid=1129&dat=19910810&id=QNc0AAAAIBAJ&sjid=aW 4DAAAAIBAJ&pg=6642,3038054 (accessed February 17, 2014), and Buzz Aldrin's memoir about life after the moon reveals a profound emptiness, often between the lines: Buzz Aldrin and Ken Abraham, *Magnificent Desolation: The Long Journey Home from the Moon* (Three Rivers Press, 2010).

146 *one-third of Americans are happy at their jobs*: "Two-Thirds America Unhappy at Job: 65% Choose New Boss over Raise Says Study by Tell YourBoss.com," *Business Wire*, http://www.businesswire.com/news/ home/20121016005065/en/Two-Thirds-America-Unhappy-Job-65-Choose-Boss (accessed March 4, 2014).

146 *a research study of white-collar employees*: The research by Teresa Amabile and Steven J. Kramer demonstrates the psychological power of progress over absolute achievements, adding to the evidence that money indeed does not buy happiness: Amabile and Kramer, *The Progress Principle: Using Small Wins to Ignite Joy, Engagement, and Creativity at Work* (Harvard Business Review Press, 2011).

148 *as addictive as cocaine*: Valerie Strauss, "Rats Find Oreos as Addictive as Cocaine—An Unusual College Research Project," *Washington Post*, October 18, 2013, http://www.washingtonpost.com/blogs/answer-sheet/ wp/2013/10/18/rats-find-oreos-as-addictive-as-cocaine-an-unusual-college-research-project/ (accessed March 4, 2014).

148 *@Oreo sent a status update*: The famous Oreo tweet, which I both loved and despised, can be found at https://twitter.com/Oreo/ status/298246571718483968.

149 Mashable *posted an article*: Amanda Wills, "Someone Give This Oreo

Employee a Raise," *Mashable*, February 3, 2013, http://mashable .com/2013/02/03/oreo-super-bowl-twitter/ (accessed February 17, 2014).

149 *525 million earned media impressions*: 360i's documentation of ongoing award and momentum making can be seen at "Dunking in the Dark," 360i, http://www.360i.com/work/oreo-super-bowl/ (accessed February 17, 2014).

150 *"Wired magazine declared Oreo"*: Ibid.

150 *"chill day. off to nyc soon for SNL week!"*: Biebs tweeted this the same day as Oreo, achieving 17,000 retweets to Oreo Cookie's 15,000 (see https://twitter.com/justinbieber/status/298136225930420224).

151 *cover a multitude of sins*: Yes, this was a bit of cringe-worthy biblical allusion.

155 *groundbreaking digital school called Khan Academy*: Sal Khan's story so far is told artfully by Clive Thompson, "How Khan Academy Is Changing the Rules of Education," *WIRED*, August 2011 (accessed February 17, 2014). While you're at it, please read Clive's book *Smarter Than You Think* (Penguin Press, 2013) sometime.

155 *a folk singer whose amazing*: The story of Sixto Rodriguez is best experienced by watching Malik Bendjelloul, *Searching for Sugar Man*, DVD, IMDb, http://www.imdb.com/title/tt2125608/ (accessed February 17, 2014). It's one of the coolest documentaries I've seen.

156 *spent years building up potential energy*: The Phan-Vasquez comparison shows how preparation affects the outcomes of lucky breaks of similar proportion. It should be noted, however, that the difference between outcomes was not simply because Phan's videos were educational, and therefore somehow more likely to be successful than Vasquez's humor. Indeed, comedy and entertainment have historically dominated YouTube charts *over* educational content. The number one female (non-popstar) YouTube channel (Phan ranks number two) at the time of this writing is that of comedian Jenna Marbles: *Jenna Marbles Blog*, http://jennamarblesblog. com/ (accessed February 17, 2014). Other massively successful YouTube stars, such as comedians the Gregory Brothers ("AutoTune the News," YouTube, http://www.youtube.com/autotunethenews), during this time period caught similar viral "breaks" and managed to turn the momentum into comedy businesses. Bear Vasquez's problem was that "Double Rainbow" was *unintentionally* funny. The category was not the defining factor in this case; it was the (lack of) preparedness to capitalize on momentum.

156 *"Success is like a lightning bolt"*: Stephanie Buck, "Michelle Phan: Behind the Makeup of YouTube's Fairy Godmother," *Mashable*, August 23, 2013, http://mashable.com/2013/08/23/michelle-phan/ (accessed February 17, 2014).

CHAPTER EIGHT: SIMPLICITY

157 *20 million premature or low-weight*: For some sad statistics about preterm births in third-world countries, see Kounteya Sinha, "India Shares Highest Preterm Birth Burden," *Times of India*, June 8, 2012, http://articles .timesofindia.indiatimes.com/2012-06-08/india/32123625_1_preterm-premature-babies-joy-lawn (accessed February 17, 2014). Studies tend to disagree slightly on the exact number of premature births that occur around the world each year (most likely due to reporting issues and varying definitions of terms), but the most reliable data seems to come from the WHO: "Preterm Birth," World Health Organization, November 2013, http://www.who.int/mediacentre/factsheets/fs363/en/ (accessed February 17, 2014).

158 *Every iteration of the incubator*: More on the development of the field of neonatology can be referenced at Alistair G. S. Philip, "The Evolution of Neonatology,"*Pediatric Research* 58, no. 4 (2005), http://www .neonatology.org/pdf/EvolutionOfNeonatology.pdf (accessed February 17, 2014).

158 *The typical incubator cost*: The *New York Times* reports that neonatal incubators range from $1,000 to $40,000: Madeline Drexler, "Looking under the Hood and Seeing an Incubator," *New York Times*, December 15, 2008, http://www.nytimes.com/2008/12/16/health/16incubators .html (accessed February 17, 2014). Jane Chen puts the typical price of a new, high-tech neonatal intensive care unit at around $20,000. I've found used incubators on eBay and from hospitals ($1,000–4,000), but in limited supply.

158 *"We started making a cheaper glass box"*: Shrabonti Bagchi, "Saving Little Lives," *Times of India*, September 19, 2011, http://epaper.timesof india.com/Repository/ml.asp?Ref=VE9JQkcvMjAxMS8wOS8xOSNBc jAwNDAw (accessed February 17, 2014).

159 *"We realized something was wrong"*: Ibid.

161 *the Latin* innovare: "Innovate," Merriam-Webster, http://www.merriam-webster.com/dictionary/innovate (accessed February 17, 2014). The classic book about disruptive innovation is, of course, Clayton M.

Christensen, *The Innovator's Dilemma* (HarperBusiness, 1997). I have drawn heavily from Christensen's ideas in various parts of this book and in my business career.

162 *Tech writer Brian Lam*: David Carr's 2012 profile of Blam will make you want to move to Hawaii, too: "Buffeted by the Web, but Now Riding It," *New York Times*, December 16, 2012, http://www.ny times.com/2012/12/17/business/media/buffeted-by-the-web-but-now-riding-it.html (accessed February 17, 2014).

162 *Blam will simply tell you*: Brian Lam's *TheWirecutter* has since expanded to several writers (to spread the load and ensure enough surf time, naturally). I actually purchased the UE Mini Boom speakers at *TheWirecutter*'s suggestion and listened to them during the making of this book. They do indeed sound good. Alexander George, "The Best Portable Bluetooth Speaker," *TheWirecutter*, November 4, 2013, http://thewirecutter.com/reviews/best-bluetooth-speaker/ (accessed February 17, 2014).

163 *"Now that I do know it"*: Arthur Conan Doyle, *A Study in Scarlet* (1887).

163 *closet was filled with dozens*: Anyone who saw Steve Jobs on stage knows the outfit: black turtleneck, blue jeans. Walter Isaacson explains the backstory in his biography: Walter Isaacson, *Steve Jobs* (Simon and Schuster, 2011).

163 *"You'll see I wear only gray or blue suits"*: Michael Lewis, "Obama's Way," *Vanity Fair*, October 2012.

164 *making lots of tiny choices depletes*: Kathleen D. Vohs, Brandon J. Schmeichel, Noelle M. Nelson, Roy F. Baumeister, Jean M. Twenge, and Dianne M. Tice, "Making Choices Impairs Subsequent Self-Control: A Limited-Resource Account of Decision Making, Self-Regulation, and Active Initiative," *Journal of Personality and Social Psychology* 94, no. 5 (2008): 883–98.

164 *doubled Apple's mouse market share*: Neil Hughes and Kasper Jade, "Magic Mouse Helps Apple Double Share of Market in 8 Weeks," *Apple Insider* (blog), December 29, 2009, http://appleinsider.com/arti cles/09/12/29/magic_mouse_helps_apple_double_share_of_market _in_8_weeks.

164 *"1,000 songs in your pocket"*: "Apple Press Info," Apple, http://www .apple.com/pr/products/ipodhistory/ (accessed February 17, 2014).

167 *kids who are tenaciously*: Focused kids win spelling bees over kids with higher IQs, according to Angela Lee Duckworth, Teri A. Kirby, Eli Tsukayama, Heather Berstein, and K. Anders Ericsson, "Deliberate Practice

Spells Success: Why Grittier Competitors Triumph at the National Spelling Bee," *Social Psychological and Personality Science* 2, no. 2 (2010): 174–81.

167 *simplicity as "the ultimate sophistication"*: This quote is attributed to Leonardo da Vinci, though the attribution has never been validated by an original source. According to Walter Isaacson, Steve Jobs was fond of the quote and it was an early Apple slogan.

CHAPTER NINE: 10X THINKING

169 *On a pleasant Sunday evening*: You can learn more about SpaceX and view footage of its launches at "SpaceX News," SpaceX, http://www .spacex.com/news (accessed February 17, 2014). The SpaceX history in this chapter comes primarily through personal interviews with former SpaceX employees, NASA historians, and aerospace academics, and from video footage of Falcon launches. An independent fact checker verified the information in my reporting and I delivered material from this chapter to Elon Musk himself for firsthand verification. (Musk did not return anything.) Two major magazine profiles of Musk provide further biographical details: Chris Anderson, "The Shared Genius of Elon Musk and Steve Jobs," *Fortune*, November 2013, and Tom Junod, "The Triumph of His Will," *Esquire*, November 2012.

171 *"I didn't think there was anything I could do"*: Chris Anderson, "Elon Musk's Mission to Mars," *Wired*, October 21, 2012, http://www.wired .com/wiredscience/2012/10/ff-elon-musk-qa/all/ (accessed February 15, 2014).

172 *NASA employed about 18,000*: NASA's headcount comes from "Space Organizations Part 1: NASA—Nasa's Workforce," Library Index, http:// www.libraryindex.com/pages/987/Space-Organizations-Part-1-NASA-NASA-S-WORKFORCE.html, and the catalog of collaborators on the Apollo project is documented by Catherine Thimmesh, *Team Moon: How 400,000 People Landed Apollo 11 on the Moon* (Houghton Mifflin Company, 2006).

172 *"To make life multiplanetary" and the continuation of "human consciousness"*: Musk often repeats these phrases in interviews, such as David Pescovitz, "Elon Musk on Making Life Multi-Planetary," *Boing Boing*, April 10, 2012, http://boingboing.net/2012/04/10/elon-musk-on-making-life-multi.html (accessed February 15, 2014), and Junod, "The Triumph of His Will."

174 *over-the-top demonstration to create buzz*: For more on Lady Gaga, Baumgartner, Alexander the Great, and 10x Storytelling, visit shanes now.com/10xstorytelling.

175 *"We choose to go to the moon"*: John F. Kennedy, "Moon Speech," Rice Stadium, Houston, September 12, 1962, http://er.jsc.nasa.gov/seh/ricetalk.htm (accessed February 15, 2014).

176 *"The Internet taught me nearly everything"*: Kosta Grammatis, *Kosta.is*, http://kosta.is/ (accessed December 20, 2013).

177 *to provide free Internet*: Kosta Grammatis's "Buy This Satellite" campaign was featured in an article by Jim Fields, "Q&A: As Egypt Shuts Down the Internet, One Group Wants Online Access for All," *Time*, January 31, 2011, http://content.time.com/time/health/article/0,8599,2045428,00.html (accessed February 17, 2014). His satellite tablet project in Dadaab, Kenya, was just commencing as this book entered production.

177 *"It's often easier"*: Astro Teller wrote this direct quote in an opinion piece for *Wired* at "Google X Head on Moonshots: 10X Is Easier Than 10 Percent," *Wired*, February 11, 2013, http://www.wired.com/opinion/2013/02/moonshots-matter-heres-how-to-make-them-happen/ (accessed February 17, 2014), and then quoted it nearly verbatim to me during a phone interview.

179 *the N-Effect*: The effect is documented in this fascinating study: Stephen M. Garcia and Avishalom Tor, "The N-Effect: More Competitors, Less Competition," *Psychological Science* 20, no. 7 (2009): 871–77. On that subject, writes Ben Nemtin on Tim Ferriss's blog, after achieving his goal of playing basketball with President Obama: "The level of competition is highest for realistic goals because most people don't set high enough goals for themselves. But not only do you statistically have a better chance of achieving what may seem like an unrealistic goal, doing so fuels you." Nemtin, "Playing B-Ball with Obama: 6 Steps to Crossing Anything Off Your Bucket List," *The Four Hour Work Week* blog, April 4, 2012, http://www.fourhourworkweek.com/blog/2012/04/04/playing-b-ball-with-obama-6-steps-to-crossing-anything-off-your-bucket-list/ (accessed February 17, 2014).

180 *Brands with lofty purposes*: Jim Stengel documents his research on the outstanding success of value-driven companies in his book *Grow: How Ideals Power Growth and Profit at the World's Greatest Companies* (Crown Business, 2011).

EPILOGUE

187 *and a rather large prison*: In case you ever get sick of Disneyland, Joliet's prison is now a vacation option: Steve Schmadeke, "Tourist Trap? Prison Park to Open," *Chicago Tribune*, July 19, 2009, http://articles.chicag otribune.com/2009-07-19/news/0907170500_1_joliet-correctional-center-inmates-tourist-attraction (accessed February 17, 2014).

187 *known as the murder capital*: It's tough to find the exact quote "murder capital" in articles about Inglewood, though locals described it as such in the late 1980s. *Los Angeles Times* reports are clear that homicide and violent crime were rising at the time: Marc Lacey, "Police Report 50% Jump in Inglewood Murders," *Los Angeles Times*, January 18, 1990, http://articles.latimes.com/1990-01-18/news/we-110_1_inglewood-police-department (accessed February 17, 2014). The song I listened to after preparing this citation: http://shanesnow.com/songZ.

198 *how many sneakers he's shipped*: In 2014, I wrote a profile of D'Wayne Edwards for *Wired*. For further reading and details on his sneaker designs and sales, see shanesnow.com/pensole.

BIBLIOGRAPHY

Agate, Nicky. *The Rough Guide to the Caribbean: More Than 50 Islands, Including the Bahamas*. Rough Guides, 2002. http://books.google.com/books?id=gWoW8qZogSQC (accessed February 15, 2014).

Aldrin, Buzz, and Ken Abraham. *Magnificent Desolation: The Long Journey Home from the Moon*. Three Rivers Press, 2010.

Amabile, Teresa, and Steven Kramer. *The Progress Principle: Using Small Wins to Ignite Joy, Engagement, and Creativity at Work*. Harvard Business Review Press, 2011.

Anderson, Heidi V. "Why Mentoring Doesn't Work."*Harvard Business Publishing Newsletters* (June 2003).

Anderson, John Lee. *Che Guevara: A Revolutionary Life*. Grove Press, 1997.

Barnett, William P., Mi Feng, and Xaioqu Luo. "Social Identity, Market Memory, and First-Mover Advantage." *Industrial and Corporate Change* 22, no. 3 (2012): 585.

Baron, Robert A. "Opportunity Recognition as Pattern Recognition: How Entrepreneurs 'Connect the Dots' to Identify." *Academy of Management Perspectives* 20, no. 1 (2006): 104–19. http://old.ied.econ.msu.ru/cmt2/lib/c/186/File/fa4_1.pdf (accessed February 16, 2014).

Bellow, Saul. *The Actual: A Novella*. Penguin Classics, 2009.

Bendjelloul, Malik. *Searching for Sugar Man* (documentary film). Red Box Films, Passion Pictures 2012. DVD, http://www.imdb.com/title/tt2125608/.

Bilton, Nick. *Hatching Twitter: A True Story of Money, Power, Friendship, and Betrayal*. Portfolio, 2013.

Bradley, Susan. *Sudden Money: Managing a Financial Windfall.* Wiley, 2000.

Campbell, Joseph. *The Hero with a Thousand Faces.* Princeton University Press, 1972.

Campitelli, Guillermo, and Fernand Gobet. "The Role of Domain-Specific Practice, Handedness, and Starting Age in Chess." *Developmental Psychology* 41, no. 1 (2007): 159–72.

Catchpole, Ken R., Marc R. De Leval, Angus McEwan, Nick Pigott, Martin J. Elliott, Annette McQuillan, Carol Macdonald, and Allan J. Goldman. "Patient Handover from Surgery to Intensive Care: Using Formula 1 Pit-Stop and Aviation Models to Improve Safety and Quality." *Pediatric Anesthesia* (2007): 470–78.

Christensen, Clayton M. *The Innovator's Dilemma.* HarperBusiness, 1997.

Chomsky, Aviva. *A History of the Cuban Revolution.* Wiley-Blackwell, 2010.

Colburn, Timothy R. *Philosophy and Computer Science.* M. E. Sharpe, 1999.

Compton, Robert. *The Finland Phenomenon* (documentary film). 2011.

Dane, Erik, Kevin W. Rockmann, and Michael G. Pratt. "When Should I Trust My Gut? Linking Domain Expertise to Intuitive Decision-Making Effectiveness." *Organizational Behavior and Human Decision Processes* 119 (2012): 187–94.

De La Pedraja, René. *Wars of Latin America, 1948–1982: The Rise of the Guerrillas.* McFarland, 2013.

Devlin, Keith. "In Math You Have to Remember, in Other Subjects You Can Think About It." *Mathematical Association of America* (June 2010). http://www.maa.org/external_archive/devlin/devlin_06_10.html (accessed February 16, 2014).

———. *The Math Gene: How Mathematical Thinking Evolved and Why Numbers Are Like Gossip.* Basic Books, 2001.

Dosal, Paul J. *Comandante Che: Guerrilla Soldier, Commander, and Strategist, 1956–1967.* Penn State University Press, 2004.

Doyle, Arthur Conan. *A Study in Scarlet.* 1887.

Duckworth, Angela Lee, Teri A. Kirby, Eli Tsukayama, Heather Berstein, and K. Anders Ericsson. "Deliberate Practice Spells Success: Why Grittier Competitors Triumph at the National Spelling Bee." *Social Psychological and Personality Science* 2, no. 2 (2010): 174–81.

Eby, Lillian T., Stacy E. McManus, Shana A. Simon, and Joyce E. A. Russell. "The Protege's Perspective Regarding Negative Mentoring Experiences: The Development of a Taxonomy." *Journal of Vocational Behavior* 57, no. 1 (2000): 1–21.

Eby, Lillian T., Tammy D. Allen, Sarah C. Evans, Thomas Ng, and David L. DuBois. "Does Mentoring Matter? A Multidisciplinary Meta-Analysis Comparing Mentored and Non-Mentored Individuals." *Journal of Vocational Behavior* 72, no. 2 (2008): 254–67.

Ellington, Aimee J. "A Meta-Analysis of the Effects of Calculators on Students' Achievement and Attitude Levels in Precollege Mathematics Classes." *Journal for Research in Mathematics Education* 34, no. 5 (2003): 433–63.

English, T. J. *Havana Nocturne: How the Mob Owned Cuba and Then Lost It to the Revolution*. William Morrow, 2008.

Finkelstein, Stacey R., and Ayelet Fishbach. "Tell Me What I Did Wrong: Experts Seek and Respond to Negative Feedback." *Journal of Consumer Research Inc.* no. 39 (2011): 22–38.

Florida, Richard. *The Rise of the Creative Class—Revisited: 10th Anniversary Edition—Revised and Expanded*, 2nd edition. Basic Books, 2012.

Frank, Robert. *Richistan: A Journey through the American Wealth Boom and the Lives of the New Rich*. Three Rivers Press, 2008.

Franklin, Benjamin. *Silence Dogood, the Busy-Body, and Early Writings*. Library of America, 2002.

Fredman, Catherine. "The IDEO Difference." *Hemispheres* (August 2002).

Freeman, Philip. *Alexander the Great*. Simon and Schuster, 2011.

Garcia, Stephen M., and Avishalom Tor. "The N-Effect: More Competitors, Less Competition."*Psychological Science* 20, no. 7 (2009): 871–77.

Gladwell, Malcolm. *Outliers: The Story of Success*. Little, Brown, 2008.

——. *The Tipping Point: How Little Things Can Make a Big Difference*. Little, Brown, 2000.

Goldbart, Stephen, and Joan Indursky DiFuria. *Affluence Intelligence: Earn More, Worry Less, and Live a Happy and Balanced Life*. Da Capo Lifelong Books, 2011.

Golder, Peter N., and Gerard J. Tellis. "Pioneer Advantage: Marketing Logic or Marketing Legend?" *Journal of Marketing Research* 30 (1993): 158–70.

Goldman, Robert, and Stephen Papson. *Nike Culture: The Sign of the Swoosh*. Sage, 1998.

Gompers, Paul, Anna Kovner, Josh Lerner, and David Scharfstein. "Performance Persistence in Entrepreneurship." *Journal of Financial Economics* 96 (2010): 18–32.

Goodwin, Doris Kearns. *Lyndon Johnson and the American Dream*. St. Martin's Griffin, 1991.

Grant, Adam. *Give and Take: A Revolutionary Approach to Success*. Viking Adult, 2013.

Guevara, Ernesto. *Che: The Diaries of Ernesto Che Guevara*. Ocean Press, 2009.

———. *Guerrilla Warfare*. BN Publishing, 2013. (Originally published in 1961).

Harris, Richard L. *Che Guevara: A Biography*. Greenwood, 2010.

Hasan, Heather. *Archimedes: The Father of Mathematics*. Rosen Publishing Group, 2006.

Homer. *The Odyssey*. Translated by Alexander Pope. George Bell & Sons. 1906.

Isaacson, Walter. *Steve Jobs*. Simon and Schuster, 2011.

Jay-Z. *Decoded*. Spiegel and Grau, 2010.

Kahneman, Daniel, and Gary Klein. "Conditions for Intuitive Expertise." *American Psychologist* 64, no. 6 (September 2009): 515–26.

Kerin, Roger A., P. Rajan Varadarajan, and Robert A. Peterson. "First-Mover Advantage: A Synthesis, Conceptual Framework, and Research Propositions." *Journal of Marketing* 56, no. 4 (1992): 33–52.

Kluger, Avraham N., and Angelo DeNisi. "The Effects of Feedback Interventions on Performance: A Historical Review, a Meta-Analysis, and a Preliminary Feedback Intervention Theory." *Psychological Bulletin* 119, no. 2 (1996): 254–84.

Lehrer, Jonah. *Imagine: How Creativity Works*. Houghton Mifflin, 2012.

Lieberman, Marvin B., and David B. Montgomery. "First-Mover Advantages." *Strategic Management Journal* no. 9 (1988): 41–58.

Lieberman, Marvin B., and David B. Montgomery. "First-Mover (Dis)Advantages: Retrospective and Link with the Resource-Based View." *Strategic Management Journal* 19 (1998): 1111–25.

MacDonald, Kyle. *One Red Paperclip: Or How an Ordinary Man Achieved His Dream with the Help of a Simple Office Supply*. Crown Archetype, 2007.

Martinez Victores, Ricardo. *La Historia de Radio Rebelde*. Editorial de Ciencias Sociales, 1978.

Martio, Olli. "Long Term Effects in Learning Mathematics in Finland—Curriculum Changes and Calculators." *Teaching of Mathematics* 12, no. 2 (2009): 51–56.

Merton, Robert K. *On the Shoulders of Giants*. Free Press, 1965.

National Research Council. *How People Learn*. Washington, DC: National Academies Press, 2000.

Newton, Isaac. Letter to Robert Hooke, February 5, 1676. http://www.isaac newton.org.uk/essays/Giants (accessed February 16, 2014).

Olson, Matthew S., and Derek van Bever. *Stall Points: Most Companies Stop Growing—Yours Doesn't Have To.* Yale University Press, 2009.

Papert, Seymour, and Idit Harel. *Constructionism.* Ablex, 1991.

Paterson, Thomas G. *Contesting Castro: The United States and the Triumph of the Cuban Revolution.* Oxford University Press, 1995.

Philip, Alistair G. S. "The Evolution of Neonatology."*Pediatric Research* 58, no. 4 (2005). http://www.neonatology.org/pdf/EvolutionOfNeonatology .pdf (accessed February 17, 2014).

Report of the 90 Day Study of Human Exploration of the Moon and Mars. NASA, 1989. http://history.nasa.gov/90_day_study.pdf.

Rhodes, James Ford. *History of the United States from the Compromise of 1850: 1864–1866.* Macmillan, 1904.

Rothwell, Jonathan, José Lobo, Deborah Strumsky, and Mark Muro. "Patenting Prosperity: Invention and Economic Performance in the United States and Its Metropolitan Areas." *Brookings* (2013).

Sahlberg, Pasi. *Finnish Lessons: What Can the World Learn from Educational Change in Finland?* Teachers College Press, 2011.

Sandberg, Sheryl. *Lean In: Women, Work, and the Will to Lead.* Knopf, 2013.

Shakespeare, William. *Julius Caesar.* http://www.shakespeare-online.com/ plays/julius_4_3.html.

Science and Engineering Indicators 2002. National Science Board, 2002.

Seifert, Charles F., and Gary Yukl. "Effects of Repeated Multi-Source Feedback on the Influence Behavior and Effectiveness of Managers: A Field Experiment." *Leadership Quarterly* 21 (2010): 856–66.

Sitkin, Sim B. "Learning through Failure: The Strategy of Small Losses." *Research in Organizational Behavior* 14 (1992): 231–66.

Sower, Victor E., Jo Ann Duffy, and Gerald Kohers. "Ferrari's Formula One Handovers and Handovers from Surgery to Intensive Care." *American Society for Quality* (August 2008).

Staats, Bradley R., KC Diwas, and Francesca Gino. "Learning from My Success and from Others' Failure: Evidence from Minimally Invasive Cardiac Surgery." *Management Science* 59, no. 11 (2013): 2435–49. http://pubson line.informs.org/doi/abs/10.1287/mnsc.2013.1720.

Stengel, Jim. *Grow: How Ideals Power Growth and Profit at the World's Greatest Companies.* Crown Business, 2011.

Stout, Nancy, and Alice Walker. *One Day in December: Celia Sanchez and the Cuban Revolution.* Monthly Review Press, 2013.

Suarez, Fernando F., and Gianvito Lanzolla. "The Role of Environmental

Dynamics in Building a First Mover Advantage Theory." *Academy of Management Review* 32, no. 2 (2007): 377–92.

Taibo, Paco Ignacio. *Guevara, Also Known as Che.* Macmillan, 1999.

Tate, Ryan. *The 20% Doctrine: How Tinkering, Goofing Off, and Breaking the Rules at Work Drive Success in Business.* HarperBusiness, 2012.

The World Factbook. Central Intelligence Agency, 2011. https://www.cia.gov/library/publications/the-world-factbook/fields/2103.html

Thimmesh, Catherine. *Team Moon: How 400,000 People Landed Apollo 11 on the Moon.* Houghton Mifflin, 2006.

Thomas, Hugh. *Cuba: La lucha por la libertad 1762–1970.* Grijalbo, 1973.

Thomas, Mike. *The Second City Unscripted: Revolution and Revelation at the World-Famous Comedy Theater.* Villard, 2009.

Thomke, Stefan. "Unlocking Innovation through Business Experimentation." *The European Business Review.* http://www.europeanbusinessreview.com/?p=8420 (accessed February 17, 2014).

Tucker, Spencer C. *Encyclopedia of Insurgency and Counterinsurgency: A New Era of Modern Warfare.* ABC-CLIO, 2013.

Underhill, Christina M. "The Effectiveness of Mentoring Programs in Corporate Settings: A Meta-Analytical Review of the Literature." *Journal of Vocational Behavior* 68 (2006): 292–307.

Underwood, Dudley. "Is Mathematics Necessary?" National Council of Teachers of Mathematics (1998). http://www.public.iastate.edu/~aleand/dudley.html (accessed February 16, 2014).

Vohs, Kathleen D., Brandon J. Schmeichel, Noelle M. Nelson, Roy F. Baumeister, Jean M. Twenge, and Dianne M. Tice. "Making Choices Impairs Subsequent Self-Control: A Limited-Resource Account of Decision Making, Self-Regulation, and Active Initiative." *Journal of Personality and Social Psychology* 94, no. 5 (2008): 883–98.

Wagner, Tony. *Creating Innovators: The Making of Young People Who Will Change the World.* Scribner, 2012.

———. *The Global Achievement Gap: Why Even Our Best Schools Don't Teach the New Survival Skills Our Children Need—and What We Can Do about It.* Basic Books, 2008.

Waitzkin, Josh. *The Art of Learning.* Free Press, 2007.

Walton, Sam, and John Huey. *Sam Walton: Made in America.* Bantam, 1993.

Wanberg, Connie R., Elizabeth T. Welsh, and John Kammeyer-Mueller. "Protégé and Mentor Self-Disclosure: Levels and Outcomes within Formal

Mentoring Dyads in a Corporate Context." *Journal of Vocational Behavior* 70, no. 2 (2007): 398–412.

Weick, Karl. "Small Wins." *American Psychologist* (1984): 40–49.

Wiener, Cat. "Winning Hearts and Minds: The Importance of Radio in the Cuban Revolutionary War" (2010). http://www.scribd.com/doc/41464197/Radio-Rebelde (accessed February 17, 2014).

Wolfe, Edward W. "What Impact Does Calculator Use Have on Test Results?" *Pearson Education Test, Measurement & Research Services Bulletin* no. 14 (2010). http://images.pearsonassessments.com/images/tmrs/tmrs_rg/Bulletin_14.pdf?WT.mc_id=TMRS_What_Impact_Does_Calculator.

World Service Conference. Narcotics Anonymous, 1981. http://amonymifoundation.org/uploads/NA_Approval_Form_Scan.pdf.

INDEX

ABOUT THE AUTHOR

Shane Snow is a journalist and entrepreneur based in New York City. In 2010 he cofounded Contently Inc., with the mission of building a better media world. He writes about technology for *Wired* magazine and *Fast Company,* and is known nationwide for speaking about the future of media. His writing has appeared in *The New Yorker,* the *Washington Post,* and *Time.*

A fellow of the Royal Society of the Arts, Snow has been named one of *Forbes* magazine's "30 Under 30 Media Innovators, " *Details* magazine's "Digital Mavericks," and *Inc.* magazine's "Coolest Entrepreneurs." *Smartcuts* is his first book.